PEOPLES, SEAS AND SHIPS

PEOPLES, SEAS AND SHIPS

by ZVI HERMAN

translated from the French by LEN ORTZEN

G. P. PUTNAM'S SONS
NEW YORK

First American Edition 1967

© 1966 Translation J. M. Dent & Sons Ltd.

All rights reserved. This book, or parts

thereof, must not be reproduced in any form

without permission.

Library of Congress Catalog Card Number: 67-23129

Printed in Israel by

Peli-P.E.C. Printing Works Ltd.

CONTENTS

ILLUSTRATIONS

PLATES

xi

In writing this book, I have simply tried to bring out the importance of the sea and the place it occupies in history and legend from the most ancient times onward. The sea has been a decisive factor in the rise and fall of peoples and kingdoms. A great and wonderful culture was born on the seashore, and the seacoast was a cradle for human evolution. The ladder of civilization, which we are still climbing, has its foot planted in salt water. It has been my aim to follow the wake of intrepid pioneer pilots who dared to set their course for unknown lands and succeeded in throwing bridges between many and diverse nations that up to then had been unaware of one another's existence. These early pilots were the heralds and bearers of human culture; they were keen merchants and ready go-betweens, not only in commerce but in the sphere of creative art and spiritual matters. It is they who began the fruitful interchange of ideas between foreign peoples, hitherto divided one from the other. It is they who planted the seed of human civilization, whether economic or spiritual, in soils which had hitherto borne no such plant. True, this seed fell sometimes on stony or drought-stricken ground, and nothing came of it. But sometimes it took root and flourished and grew into a tree whose mighty trunk was crowned with splendid foliage.

It is the opinion of many eminent historians that the phases of rapid cultural and economic advance that occur sporadically in history are identical with those in which dominant peoples or conquering powers maintained direct contact with the sea, and conversely phases of decadence and stagnation occurred when, and only when, the contact between such peoples and powers and the sea was weakened or severed.

The doctrine preached by this school, which one might call thalassologists, or people who place stress on the significance of the sea and the part it has played in the crystallization of human history, is, without doubt, too extreme. Nevertheless, we should recognize that this doctrine rests on pretty solid foundations.

What method have I followed? Any attempt to describe a certain period of history always comes up against one special problem—how to present events that developed simultaneously and are obviously linked together and whose results are interdependent. It is impossible to give a horizontal picture of historical facts covering a vast expanse of space and time. This would require no mean powers of description over and above the composing of an acceptable synthesis of events. But even a historian whose talents combine these two rare qualities seldom achieves anything more than an overcrowded, confused, and somewhat blotchy canvas, when he tries to paint this sort of scene.

For this reason I have chosen what may be called the vertical method of description, because my aim throughout has been to bring into relief, in a clear crystallized form, the part that the sea has played in the history of antiquity. A superabundance of detail, tending to link the facts together simultaneously, would doubtless have tended to obscure the aim I have set myself. It is evident that the maritime events of Egypt are closely linked to the history of the Phoenicians and the Greeks. More than this, the fortunes of the Phoenicians are tangled and plaited with the life of the Hellenic peoples. It is possible that in adopting this method, I had to forgo perfection in other historical respects. But then I am not a professional historian, and this work has no pretensions to be a complete and specialized scientific project. I hope—and it is my only hope—that professional historians will not cast too many stones at me if by chance this book should fall into their hands and they should deign to accord it their critical interest.

It goes without saying that in the choice of events to be

recorded, I have been indebted to none but my own judgment, and if events of minor importance have thereby acquired, under my pen, an exaggerated significance, or if I have omitted facts that the professional historian considers eminently important, why then, so much the worse. I have brought this book to a close with the fall of Tyre, without embarking on the legends, the expeditions and the other feats of her marvelous daughter, Carthage. During the last 200 years of the reign of the mother city, Carthage in her own right became a rich and important seagoing power, richer and more important than the source from which she had been colonized. But I have avoided, or rather have deliberately abstained, in conformity with the method which I have adopted, from mixing events and states, and I have not committed myself to interlaced descriptions that were not essential to my purpose. For this reason also, I have referred only incidentally to the great naval wars between the Greeks and the Persians, which decided in their time the fate and the development of European civilization. These are episodes in the history of Greek seafaring. I hope that I shall be spared one day to write the wonderful chapter of Greek seafaring, just as I hope that one day I shall write the history of Carthagenian shipping — the story of the great Lady of the Sea in the West.

It has not been my wish to cumber my text with notes and cross-references that might impede rapid reading. But at the end of the volume you will find a reasonably copious list of books in English on this and allied subjects, which he who wishes to enlarge his knowledge of the matters on which I write may consult to his profit and entertainment.

And now I commit this my book to whatever fates await it in the English language. I launch it thus, not without some knowledge of its faults and deficiencies, on an unknown course. If it succeeds in arousing a little interest in the navigation of

Biblical times, I shall have been sufficiently rewarded. And if some other writer, attracted to the subject by its appeals, were to devote himself to a much deeper and more methodical study of questions concerning the sea and the part it plays in the culture and the progress of mankind in general and of Israel in particular, I should consider myself doubly rewarded.

The Queen of Punt

Chapter 1

THE BEGINNINGS

It is generally supposed that primitive man was first inspired to travel by the desire to trade, and it may well have been the discovery of fire, or rather the means of having fire, that first led him to begin bartering. We do not know how primitive man came to understand that the leaping flames could make life less difficult and protect him from dangers. But we do know that one day he noticed that certain hard stones struck together could be made to produce fire. This was a discovery of the highest importance. There were soon "industrial centers" established in and around the areas where this stone was found, and the first tribes of craftsmen were specialists in the making of flint weapons and tools. It became well worthwhile to undertake long and hazardous journeys in order to obtain this inestimable treasure —the hard, cold stone that contained the mysterious power of giving fire.

In the abnormally hot summer of 1854, which caused the level of some of the Swiss lakes to drop considerably, the remains of prehistoric settlements were brought to light. The remains were very well preserved. Some of the buildings were on piles and had been connected to dry land by narrow bridges. The most interesting discovery made by archaeologists was on the banks of Lake Neuchâtel. The drop in the level of the water had revealed a number of Stone Age implements, including some made of that wonderful hard substance which produced fire, and chemical analysis of the silica proved that it could have originated in only one place—Rügen Island, in the Baltic.

Other objects, which must have been carried even longer distances, have also been found. For instance, shells from the Indian Ocean and the Red Sea have been discovered in tombs dating back to the Mesolithic and Neolithic periods in Germany, Britain, and Sweden. By what combination of circumstances, one wonders, did the shells reach those distant lands?

Excavations in Mesopotamia have revealed buildings about six thousand years old that had doors and beams made of

1

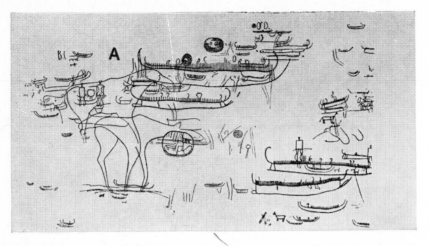

**Bronze Age rock drawing
showing boats**

teak—a tree that grows only in the Far East and in West Africa. It is highly improbable that there was any contact between Mesopotamia and West Africa in those ancient times, so the teak must have been brought from the Far East. But how? Since it could not have gone overland, across the Himalayas, the sea passage was the only possible way.

A number of products of the Indies have been discovered during excavations in East Africa on sites dating back to 2000 B.C. Modern man, convinced of his superior knowledge and progress, finds it difficult to believe that his Neolithic ancestors could have made sea voyages of 1,500 miles and more. Considerable knowledge of prevailing winds and of the currents would have been necessary. Many questions, then, remain to be answered.

The exchanges of implements, weapons and building material were followed by the bartering of foodstuffs, and this very necessary trade led more than anything to the development of communications. Toward the end of the Middle Ages the shortest sea route to the East Indies was being sought in order to bring to Europe spices, which were in great demand. Man had soon learned to flavor his food; it had little taste otherwise. Besides, at that period the salt that was so necessary to preserve foodstuffs for the winter was in short supply. The oldest known salt mines were at Hallstatt, in the Austrian province of Styria; the area is still known as the Salzkammergut (salt mines district). Salt was first extracted there about 2500 B.C., but ever since the earliest times men have gone to immense efforts and undertaken incredibly long journeys to

2

obtain supplies of salt, which counted as wealth. Wars have broken out over this vital mineral. In this respect, modern times have brought nothing new; instead of fighting over salt, men now fight over oil.

Prehistoric man made long journeys for more surprising reasons than to obtain implements and foodstuffs. The desire for ornamentation, for self-adornment, was a considerable factor in the development of trade and the growth of civilization. After having discovered the uses of fire and of salt and all that was primordial to enable him to exist in a hostile nature, man then discovered amber, and with it came the desire to adorn himself. In making jewelry and ornaments, he was responding to a basic instinct of the human race. Feminine elegance in prehistoric times can hardly be compared with that of today; nevertheless, even in the second millennium B.C. women pos-

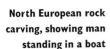

North European rock carving, showing man standing in a boat

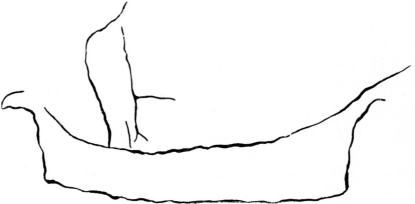

sessed what was required for their coquetry, as is evident from our knowledge of, for instance, the Cretan civilization from 2500 to 1500 B.C. Amber jewelry was the fashion (many brooches, rings, bracelets and necklaces have been found in graves of the Minoan period), and amber, as is well known, comes only from the shores of the Baltic. This yellow translucent substance was believed to have magical properties, and amulets of it were worn to charm away certain evils. The name "electron" was given to it by the Greek philosopher Thales of Miletus, because of its strange power of becoming electrified when rubbed. Such a phenomenon is easily explained today, but how were the ancients to know that there is nothing supernatural about it?

Many legends grew up around the origins of amber, but one thing was certain and evident: women were passionately fond of amber jewelry, and long journeys, real expeditions, had to

The Great Pyramid of Cheops, which took 100,000 slaves twenty years to build, using 6,000,000 tons of stone

be undertaken to obtain supplies of the valuable substance. Just think of a Cretan, for instance, setting out with all his baggage—a considerable amount, for he had to take merchandise to barter with—sailing up the Adriatic to where Venice now stands, and then beginning the interminable overland journey to Jutland. What a round trip in order to satisfy the demands of fashion! However, after a time a large market grew up near the port of Aquileia, at the head of the Adriatic. Merchandise from the Mediterranean countries was there exchanged for wares from the north, especially for amber, which was brought almost invariably by the same route—the amber route, as it came to be

4

called. It went right across central Europe and, like the silk route across Asia, always had several merchant convoys traveling its length.

The early routes of communication thus owed much to the demands for amber and, later, silk. Indeed, it might not be too much to say that the development of trade routes and the growth of civilization were due in a large measure to the fashionable tastes and elegance of Cretan and Egyptian women.

Expert opinion is divided over the question of when primitive man turned from stone to metal. Some archaeologists give 6000 B.C. as the beginning of the Bronze Age, while others place it between 5000 and 4500 B.C. However, these dates can mean little when the whole length of the prehistoric age is still not known. In 1958 a human skeleton was discovered near Grosseto, central Italy, by Professor Hirzeller, who claimed it was at least a million years old. Whether or not we accept the anthropologist's conclusions, his estimation proves that man preceded the monkey and that the known period of the history of mankind is relatively short.

Nor is it known how primitive man first discovered that by mixing tin with copper he obtained an ideal metal for making weapons, ornaments and cooking utensils. The discovery of bronze probably came by chance, as is true of so many of man's discoveries. The area where it occurred—where this alloy, which was to transform man's life, was first produced—is another question on which experts are divided.

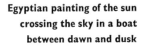

Egyptian painting of the sun crossing the sky in a boat between dawn and dusk

An invention even more wonderful and important to man than bronze began to spread at about the same period, a novelty owed entirely to the inventive genius of man—writing.

Trading developed greatly with the discovery of bronze. In areas where copper was found, towns grew up and became prosperous and important. The men who engaged in the trade of carrying copper and tin amassed great wealth. Bronze was transported by sea from Tartessus, on the Atlantic coast of southern Spain, to Thebes, 400 miles up the Nile; tin from Britain to Crete and Troy; from Sumer and Elam (southern Mesopotamia) to Greece. Bronze became a necessity. Whole fleets were built to carry it. Wars were fought because of it.

In those times it was not a case of "trade following the flag" but the opposite—trade opened the way to colonization and conquest. The need to arm ships came with the growth of the bronze-carrying trade.

Some specialists believe that bronze was first produced in Aram-Naharayim (Babylonia) and in the Nile valley, during the fourth millennium B.C. Copper was found in abundance in those regions, which have always been thought of as cradles of humanity and the birthplaces of great civilizations. If we follow the routes by which these civilizations spread over the known world, we find that they lead down to the sea.

Chapter 2

THE MYSTERIOUS "GOD'S LAND"

Before turning to Egypt and its mysteries, a word must be said about a neighboring civilization, one of the earliest in the world and one which shed a glorious light for centuries—the Babylonian, more particularly the Sumerian. At a very early time the inhabitants of the land between the Tigris and the Euphrates had a wide knowledge of many skills and were trading with countries to the east. They imported a variety of materials, teak in particular, with which they built their temples and palaces. The code of laws of King Hammurabi of Babylon (c. 1704-1662 B.C.) regulated trade. It is possible that wheeled vehicles were in use there long before they appeared elsewhere, and an early knowledge of sailing appears likely, to judge from excavations carried out at Eridu (which, in antiquity, was a port at the head of the Persian Gulf).

There is still a great deal to be learned about the Babylonian civilization. Archaeologists who are continuing the work begun by Sir Leonard Woolley have many mysteries to solve.

Among all the many inscriptions discovered in Egypt during Bonaparte's expedition and his conquest of the country, there is one that gives a complete understanding of the reason why those wonders of the world, the pyramids, were built.

> He will go on living even as Osiris is living. He will not die, even as Osiris is not dead. He will not wither,

7

even as Osiris has not withered. Even as a new breath of life revived the body of Osiris, so will the gods bring him back to life and set him among them.

The heavenly gates have opened before thee; the great bolts have been drawn. Ra is standing there; he takes thee by the hand and leads thee to the saint who is in the heavens and seats thee upon the throne of Osiris. Now thou art on this royal throne which is made of bronze for thee to reign over the great ones. The servants of the god are standing behind thee and the nobles of the god before thee, calling to thee: "Come, O god, come and sit on the throne of Osiris!" Isis speaks to thee, and Nephthys wishes thee well. The great ones approach and prostrate themselves before thee, kiss the ground at thy feet. Thou art protected here. Thou art dressed as a god, and hast been given the appearance of Osiris. Thou occupiest the throne of the first among those of the West. Thou wilt be likened to him among the great ones forever. Thou art ordering thy house so that it prosper after thee.

In Egyptian mythology, men revolted against the god Ra, who reigned over the earth, and in his wrath he sent a goddess called Hathor to destroy them. But while she was carrying out his orders, the god changed his mind and, with aversion in his soul, left the earth astride a celestial cow. Thus Ra ascended to the heavens and reigned henceforth over men in the shape of the sun. He had two vessels for his journey across the firmament. He used one before noon and the other after. It was in the latter that he journeyed to the extreme west, to the Cheol—the kingdom of the dead—taking a little joy, warmth and light to the souls stripped of their bodies.

The ancient Egyptians obviously believed in the continuance of life after death and that their king would be reunited with the gods. His tomb had to be large and splendid, furnished with everything necessary to ensure his safety and comfort in the afterlife, and strong enough to protect his body from tomb robbers and to stand for all time. Thus were the giant pyramids built.

Many theories have been advanced about the mathematics of their dimensions, but what concerns us here is their construction. Experts estimate that about 2,300,000 blocks of stone were used to build the largest of them all, the Pyramid of Cheops, just outside Cairo. The average weight of each block being two and a half tons, a total of nearly six million tons was

8

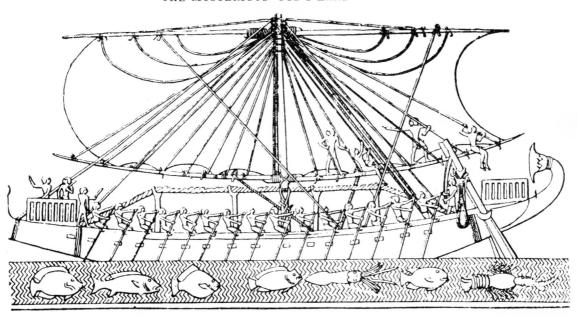

**One of the ships belonging to
the fleet of Queen Hatshepsut**

therefore carried to the site. And that is not counting the marble and the granite used for covering and decorating the pyramid.

Most of the material came from quarries in Upper Egypt, near the first cataract, and from quarries just south of Giza. But the Egyptians opened new quarries wherever stone or granite was found. It all was brought down the Nile on rafts and in long, flat-bottomed boats, with a low prow and stern that facilitated the loading and unloading of the huge blocks. This intense activity on the great river lasted for twenty years, the time taken to build the Great Pyramid of Cheops.

The ancient Egyptians sailed their boats not only on the Nile, but also in the Mediterranean, the Red Sea, and even the Indian Ocean, for we know that they reached "God's Land," or the Land of Punt.

As with all Eastern religions, the priests of ancient Egypt had need of vast quantities of aromatic plants to burn as incense. Frankincense, myrrh and lavender were also used for embalming purposes. The long and exacting task of the embalmers—of which Herodotus has left us a somewhat sickening description—called for a great number of spices and scented ointments. Their formulas and the embalming methods employed are now un-

9

known, despite Herodotus' description. Embalming is practiced today, admittedly, but usually by means of arterial injection. And whatever the means employed to preserve corpses today, we shall never know if it is as effective as that of the ancient Egyptians.

To the needs of the priests were added those of the cosmetic trade. Beauty products were by no means unknown to Egyptian women in the time of the pharaohs. They applied scented creams and a bluish makeup and lengthened or darkened their eyebrows and eyelashes by the use of powdered antimony. Colored powder —red and white— was also among their beauty preparations and was in great demand. Their hairstyles were very complicated, calling for much skill and artistic arrangement. Recent excavations have revealed numerous aids and implements that point to an advanced cosmetic civilization.

Unfortunately, none of these beauty products—which were very expensive—came from Egypt itself, but had to be obtained from other countries. The cosmetic trade and the priests and embalmers were entirely dependent on imports, chiefly from Arabia, especially the Yemen and the Hadhramaut regions.

Were the demands so great and the cost so high, one wonders, that it was worth seeking fresh sources of supply? An answer has been provided by the ancient Egyptians themselves. They were an order-loving people, and bureaucracy flourished in their time. From the "books" of the temple of Amon-Ra, which were discovered during excavations at Thebes, we learn that in 1200 B.C. the temple used 2,189 large jars and 304,093 bushels of frankincense for religious purposes alone. All that for one temple in a single year! Such figures defy the imagination. The total amount of incense burned and cosmetics used must have been colossal in any one year. The cost of it all to Egypt made going on long and dangerous expeditions to other lands, in order to break the monopoly of southwestern Arabia, more than worthwhile.

The wonderful Land of Punt, the country of incense trees, was first visited by Egyptians under the reign of Sahura II of the fifth dynasty. This pharaoh seems to have been daring and enterprising. He extended Egypt's domination along the shores of the Mediterranean, as well as sending a fleet to the Land of Punt. A bas-relief of the period, on the temple at Aboukir, shows for the first time some Phoenician or Semite prisoners being carried in four Egyptian ships.

10

Sahura's fleet returned with 80,000 measures of oil of myrrh, 6,000 ingots of silver and gold, and 2,600 balks of ebony—a rare and precious wood. The expedition had obviously been most successful, and it was probably not the first of its kind. During the reign of Sahura there was almost constant contact between Egypt and "God's Land," the former importing luxury foodstuffs and even dwarfs. The ancient Egyptians were very fond of dwarfs and regarded them much as royal jesters were regarded in medieval times.

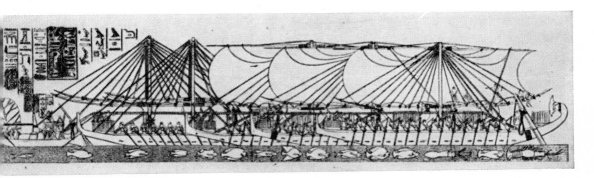

A squadron of five ships belonging to the fleet of Queen Hatshepsut (fresco in temple at Deir el-Bahri)

There was therefore every reason for considering as "the country of the gods" a land that had such an abundance of myrrh, incense, gold, silver, ebony, panthers and dwarfs.

The pharaohs of the fifth and sixth dynasties made great efforts to develop trade relations with the Land of Punt. On Elephantine Island, in the Nile above Thebes, the tomb of a man named Knemhotep has been found. He was not a member of the ruling class nor did he hold a high military rank. He was merely a son of the people. But his function in life had nevertheless merited a special tomb with an inscription, an honor usually accorded only to kings and, occasionally, high-ranking officers. Knemhotep had been a sailor and had made the voyage to Punt eleven times, under his captain, Koui, and the eleven voyages had taken place without any incident.

The expedition to Punt about which we possess interesting and detailed descriptions was organized and financed by the celebrated Queen Hatshepsut. She was one of the most fascinating figures in the history of Egypt—and not just Egypt, for she has a prominent place among the illustrious women of all times.

11

She was certainly the first eminent woman in history to cope with the political strife of her time, and she showed that a woman was capable of emerging victorious from a long and dangerous party struggle.

Queen Hatshepsut overcame many difficulties and obstacles and had the courage to vie with men in the exercise of power. Despite her responsibilities, she never lost her feminine grace and charm and always showed a lively interest in the arts, architecture, the peaceful life and ... love. This exceptional monarch was an amazing mixture of boldness and gentleness. With her beauty and intelligence and her many natural gifts, she had the necessary shrewdness to see her through the most complicated intrigues.

Her memory was deliberately tarnished by her successors, especially Tuthmosis III, who is considered one of the greatest pharaohs and the founder of the Egyptian empire. He even had the tablets recording Hatshepsut's achievements destroyed, and profiles of her on reliefs were defaced. How deep his hatred must have been to go to the extent of profaning the memory of a pharaoh residing in the kingdom of the dead!

Hatshepsut was a descendant, through her mother, of the celebrated Queen Nefertiti, wife of the founder of the eighteenth dynasty who came to power at a confused period in Egyptian history. A warlike and primitive people from western Asia, the Hyksos, had imposed their rule upon Egypt around the year 1750 B.C. and were not finally expelled until two centuries later, about 1580 B.C. The pharaohs of the seventeenth dynasty revived the ancient traditions, and all traces of the hated foreign influence were soon eliminated. By the time of Tuthmosis I, the third pharaoh of the eighteenth dynasty, the central authority was again firmly established and a period of order and prosperity had begun. Military expeditions and conquests were being undertaken.

Tuthmosis I had two wives — Princess Achmose, who was of royal blood, and Mutnoufrath. He had a daughter, Hatshepsut, by the former, and a son, who was also named Tuthmosis, by the latter.

It was customary for a pharaoh, when he felt old age approaching, to designate his successor and to hand over to him most of the royal prerogatives. Tuthmosis named Princess Hatshepsut to succeed him. She was then twenty-four, intelligent, strong-minded and energetic, but nevertheless a woman. A female pharaoh! Never had such a thing been known. In order to strengthen her position she was married to her half-brother,

Tuthmosis II. He soon died. Whether it was from natural causes or as a result of his wife's plotting is not known. In any case, Hatshepsut was able to marry again. Her second husband was another Tuthmosis who became known as Tuthmosis III. There was some mystery about his origins. He was believed to be a son of Tuthmosis I by one of his concubines. The young Tuthmosis had been supported by the legitimist party, which maintained that a king of Egypt must be of royal blood, and so he was obliged to associate Hatshepsut with the power he held. He then allied himself with the aged Tuthmosis I, but Hatshepsut soon gathered all authority into her own hands and reigned supreme over the country. She succeeded in gaining the support of the priests and the aristocracy, with the consequence that all influential circles ranged themselves on her side, and Tuthmosis III found himself relegated to a subordinate position.

A good description of her has been left to us by Tuthmosis I's chief engineer (who probably had little reason for liking her). He made a passing reference to Tuthmosis III, calling him "the master seated on the throne of him who had sired him" (a diplomatic way of putting it!), and went on: "His sister Hatshepsut directs the Two Lands [Upper and Lower Egypt] according to her plans; and Egypt works for this excellent child of god without raising its head. She is the chain attached to the prow of the southern ship, the anchor of the southern people, the cable attached to the stern of the northern ship. She is the lady who commands and whose excellent intentions and speeches give satisfaction to both lands."

Queen Hatshepsut's activities fully justified the comparison to the anchor of the ship of state.

There were undoubtedly economic reasons for the Queen's sending her great expedition to the Land of Punt. She had started on a vast building program for which money was needed. The Land of Punt was rich, and much gold was found there. But political reasons and the need to enhance her prestige also played a part in her decision. Religious motives apparently came into it as well. In the temple of Amon, during her investiture, she had heard a voice telling her "to seek out the routes leading to Punt, to reopen the paths to myrrh, and to send delegations by sea and by land to bring back the marvels of God's Land."

So Queen Hatshepsut fitted out five large ships, each of thirty oars, and in 1495 (or 1493) B.C. they passed into the Red Sea by way of the canal through the Wadi Tamilat. This canal that linked the Nile with the Red Sea was the first and very early version of the Suez Canal. The reliefs and inscriptions of the temple at Deir el-Bahri record the progress of the great expedition. The ships are shown carrying Egyptian goods and products, to be used as barter and for gifts. The cargo even includes a large statue of the Queen, presumably to enable the people of Punt to appreciate her magnificence and beauty.

The fleet reached its destination without incident, and the Egyptians were given a most friendly welcome. It was in fact an historic occasion, for more than five centuries had passed since an Egyptian fleet had last visited Punt. The delegation was received by King Perehou and his wife. She was small and had short, fat legs. The Egyptian sculptor was obviously impressed by the proportions of her plump, rounded figure, and likened her a little to the women shown on Assyrian reliefs. As she was queen in her own country, she must certainly have been thought beautiful—proving that appreciation of feminine beauty is entirely relative.

The expedition appears to have been a great commercial success. Queen Hatshepsut proudly recorded on the walls of the temple of Deir el-Bahri: "Our ships were filled with all marvelous things from Punt; the scented wood of God's Land, piles of resin, myrrh, green balsam trees, ebony, ivory, gold, cinnamon, incense, eye-coloring, monkeys with long tails, gray dogs and panther skins. No other pharaoh before me," she added without false modesty, "had such things brought to him."

The thirty-one balsam trees were planted on the terraces of the temple at Deir el-Bahri, which was dedicated to Amon-Ra and Queen Hatshepsut. And this too was recorded: "I created Punt in his gardens, as he [the god] had commanded me. It is a vast garden, so that I can walk about in it."

The joy of the crews—and the pride of their Queen—when the ships reached the port of Kosseir on the Red Sea can well be imagined. Never within living memory had an expedition returned from overseas with so many rare and wonderful things. The financial and propaganda aims of the Queen in organizing the expedition had been fulfilled, and the directive from the gods had been faithfully carried out. If, in addition, she had hoped that the expedition would increase her prestige, to the detriment of Tuthmosis III, then it could be counted a complete success.

Despite the amount of detail we have about the expedition, there is no description of the Land of Punt that enables us to fix its geographical situation with any certainty. Egyptologists

14

The King and Queen of Punt receiving an Egyptian delegation

thought at one time that it was the Hadhramaut region of southern Arabia. Later, opinion inclined toward Eritrea or Somaliland. The theory was also advanced that it was on the west coast of India. But the details of the land and its inhabitants recorded by the ancient Egyptians removed all possibility of any of these theories being correct. The mystery might still remain (like the identification of Ophir, a land that the Hebrews and Phoenicians sailed to in the time of King Solomon) were it not for a chance discovery by a German professor of chemistry. He was analyzing some cosmetics found in a casket which had belonged to an Egyptian princess of the sixth dynasty (2400–2300 B.C.), and to his great surprise discovered they contained antimony. This bluish-white metallic substance was used to make kohl, the powder with which women in the East darkened their eyelids. But antimony was not found in Egypt, and the antimony mines in Persia and Turkey were not discovered until very much later than 2300 B.C., nor were those in North Africa. The only region in Africa where antimony was found was the southern part of the country which came to be known as Rhodesia. If the Egyptians used antimony in the time of the sixth dynasty, it could have come only from Rhodesia.

At that period the Egyptians were making frequent voyages to the Land of Punt—Knemhotep the sailor, who visited it eleven times, lived in that period—and the distance is known

15

to have been some four thousand miles. To make a round-trip sea voyage of eight thousand miles at that time was a great achievement. Nevertheless, there are good grounds for the support of this theory. The Egyptians did not, of course, make the long voyage merely to help their cosmetic trade. In antiquity as at all times—even in the latter part of the last century—men faced danger and privation in search of gold, and the pharaohs were more anxious for gold than any other thing. There were also the demands for myrrh and incense. Besides, it was not the pharaohs who were risking their lives in making the journey, but their subjects, and they mattered little.

In ancient times there were gold mines being worked in what is now Rhodesia. According to reputable sources, Ramses III maintained a large colony of Egyptians there (about 1190 B.C.), to work some of the mines and send the gold to Egypt. The fort at Zimbabwe, whose considerable ruins appear out of place in those parts of Africa (south of the Zambezi), is thought by some experts to have been built by Ramses' "colonists." It was later extended by the Phoenicians to protect their mining settlement against the Sudanese.

There is also the fact that the bas-reliefs on the temple at Deir el-Bahri which record Queen Hatshepsut's expedition show the people of Punt as having physical characteristics similar to Hottentots. The women, the Queen of Punt in particular, are shown with a large posterior that makes them remarkably like present-day Hottentot women.

What kind of ships, then, did the ancient Egyptians have, to enable them to make such long and daring voyages?

PLATE 1

Egyptian funerary ship, 2000 B.C.

The Maritime Museum at Haifa and also the British Museum exhibit many of these funeral barques in the excellent state of preservation in which they were found in Egyptian tombs.

According to the belief of the ancient Egyptians, the human soul, after the death of the body, follows the sun in its eternal course, and for this reason they took care to bury close to the corpse of the deceased a boat or ship, or model thereof, with a crew of dolls. This boat is rigged with a V-shaped mast which would normally carry a sail. Forward of the mast three rowers can be seen who are slaves, together with a coxswain, who is giving them the time. The steersman is sitting in the stern operating the double steering oars. Amidships is an awning giving shade to a chair or throne which the dead man should occupy.

The construction of this vessel has been strongly influenced by the boats which were made of bundles of papyrus reed, and this influence is reflected in the profiles of the prow and the stern, even to the extent of having the sternpost and the head of the prow carved in the form of a papyrus flower.

PLATE I

Egyptian funerary ship, 2000 B.C.

Building a ship in ancient Egypt

Chapter 3

EGYPTIAN SHIPS AND CONQUESTS

Egypt, wrote Herodotus, is a gift of the Nile. A true phrase, and a highly significant one, for the great river has set its stamp on the economic, political and cultural development of Egypt. It is the source of the country's life and the basis of her natural wealth, bringing down mud and silt from the distant mountains irrigating the valley, and turning desert wastes into fertile land. The Nile has always been the chief and most practical means of communication, linking Upper Egypt with the Delta and the Mediterranean. Many towns have grown up along its banks.

It was, then, only natural for the Nile—navigable practically throughout the year—to have become Egypt's most important trade route. The products and wares of Nubia, the Sudan, and Abyssinia reached the Egyptian markets by way of the Nile. From the Delta, Egyptian and Cretan ships—and, later, Phoenician and Greek—could sail up the river when it was in flood. Given such favorable circumstances, it was only natural that the Egyptians should have mastered the art of boatbuilding at a very early date.

Their first efforts were limited to river floats made of papyrus and reeds, which they learned to shape like a boat. Although strong enough to carry a man, this rudimentary craft was of very limited use. It could not travel far or transport anything heavy.

17

Fishing from papyrus boats

Later, rafts were built. By the time of Cheops, as we know from bas-reliefs, boats existed that were capable of carrying heavy blocks of stone. Their low prow and stern facilitated the loading and unloading, which were done with the aid of ropes and levers. These boats were quite small at first (little more than punts, in fact), and were rowed by three or four men on each side, standing upright. They were made of short lengths of wood, but had no strakes from stem to stern to strengthen the whole. Nor did they have a keel, and this meant that when a boat was riding the waves, all the weight was concentrated in the beam —the only part actually in the water. At such a critical moment a boat could break in two, which happened fairly often. The Phoenicians were the first to overcome this disadvantage by fitting keels to their boats.

Egypt was a great power in very early times. The peoples established along the Nile became unified and created a major civilization and a great empire. But what led these tribes to become united? Why there in the long Nile valley, and not in other regions with similar geographical features and climatic conditions? One thing is clear—the political development of Egypt brought about an economic development, as a high level of culture naturally produces many material demands. To meet these economic, religious and cultural demands, the Egyptians developed their commercial organization, and this in turn led them to improve and increase their merchant fleet. There were, of course, military and strategic reasons too. The rulers of Egypt realized that sea communications were more convenient, faster, and less costly than overland routes.

There is strong evidence that Snefru, a pharaoh of the third dynasty (around 2900 B.C.), had a fairly large fleet for carrying soldiers and goods on the Nile. Some of these boats were one

18

hundred and fifty feet long. However, the Egyptians did not remain mere river sailors. Before long, they had acquired sufficient knowledge to venture out to sea.

Egypt has no trees suitable for building boats, or even furniture (the many palm and acacia trees are of no use in this respect), so the Egyptians have always been obliged to obtain their timber from other lands. Like many developing countries since, Egypt felt the need of overseas markets very early in her history. But until she had a seagoing merchant fleet of her own, she was under the unpleasant necessity of being dependent upon seafarers to whom ancient inscriptions refer, with some disdain, as Peoples of the Sea. Little is known about them, but in view of the trade intercourse that existed between Egypt and Crete, they very likely came from that island, or from those in the Aegean.

The Egyptians soon realized that their river punts needed some form of steering. It was probably not they who invented the rudder, but they did develop its use. At first, a length of wood was fixed over the stern, and in time this took the shape of a long paddle. Boats became longer and wider too, giving more space for the oars, and the rowers were able to sit down to their task.

The greatest help to navigation was undoubtedly the invention of the sail—an innovation as wonderful as that of steam. What enormous progress had been made! Instead of manpower,

Cargo boat on the Nile

boats could be propelled by one of the forces of nature. Moreover, much greater distances could be covered under sail than with oars. A boat carrying a sail had possibilities exceeding one with as many as thirty experienced rowers. But the best arrangement (for the Mediterranean) was soon found to be a boat with oars and sail. This combination prevailed for thousands of years. Galleys were still in use in the eighteenth century A.D.—there are no more conservative people than sailors and shipbuilders!

The Egyptian sail was square, or rectangular, whereas all other Mediterranean seafarers used a triangular sail. Another difference was that the Egyptian mast (the sail was slung from two yards at the top, of equal length either side) was not a single length of wood like that of other boats sailing the Mediterranean, but was formed by two separate lengths joined at the top (an inverted V), and was stepped amidships. This is curious, and one wonders why the Egyptians did not follow the lead of the Cretan and Aegean seamen, with whom they had maritime intercourse and who were more experienced in open-sea navigation. The only other area of the world where the double mast is known to have been used was in the Far East. A coincidence, perhaps. Or could it be that relations existed between Egypt and the Far East at a very remote time, and the shape of the early Egyptian mast and sail thereby resulted? No evidence of any kind is available, but here is a new field of investigation waiting to be explored.

The Egyptian double mast eventually gave way to a single one, through Phoenician influence in particular, but the square or rectangular sail continued to be carried.

The Cretans and the Greeks apparently used a square mainsail and a triangular topsail, which were secured with ropes. Their ships moved at a good speed when a strong breeze was blowing, and, when it dropped, the rowers supplied the necessary force. The Egyptians do not appear to have been very adept at sailing; it was the Phoenicians and the Greeks, rather, who learned best how to handle sails and to navigate.

Egypt, as already mentioned, was lacking in timber suitable for boatbuilding. The early punts, or skiffs, were made of short lengths of wood; and the joins, which often leaked, were stanched with papyrus. They could hardly be called seaworthy. Rough water could easily stave them in. Numerous bas-reliefs of ancient temples and palaces show the methods of the Egyptian boatbuilders to be very primitive. There also exists an interesting description given by Herodotus (Book II, Chapter 96) of a Nile boatyard which he visited during one of his many journeys:

Egyptian yacht

Boats for carrying goods on the Nile are made of acacia wood, which is similar to the lotus tree of Cyrenaica and exudes gum. The Egyptians cut lengths of about three feet, fasten them together with long pegs to make the shell of the boat, then fit the beams across. No sides are put on; the joins are merely stuffed with papyrus from the inside. A paddle is inserted through the stern to act as a rudder. The mast is of acacia wood too; the sail is made of papyrus. These boats are unable to sail upstream unless there is a strong wind, but have to be hauled from the bank. When going downriver they are carried by the current, but each boat has to use a "floating anchor": a raft made of tamarisk wood tied with reeds and carrying a small sail of plaited bulrushes is put in the water ahead of the boat, attached to it by ropes, while a heavy stone (about one hundred pounds' weight) with a hole in it is dropped astern, also attached to the boat by a rope. The swift current carries along the raft drawing the boat, and the stone acts as a brake and keeps the boat on a straight course. There are many such boats on the Nile; some can carry a great amount of cargo.

To judge from Herodotus, navigation on the Nile in his time (fifth century B.C.) must have been a most complicated affair.

Temple of Queen Hatshepsut
at Deir el-Bahri

The ancient historian wrote about it at length, as the method employed was unknown to the Greeks. And to judge from his description of boatbuilding, the techniques of the Egyptian workmen had not changed in thousands of years. Nevertheless they succeeded in building boats in which very long voyages were made, voyages of thousands of miles and which lasted several years ...

The Egyptians used cedar from Lebanon and Syria to build their fleet, a timber of excellent quality that was imported in great quantities for several centuries. In the time of Ramses III, the Egyptians were building ships more than two hundred feet long. The pharaohs were not satisfied with just a large merchant fleet. They had pleasure boats built for themselves, and some of these "yachts" had several decks and were fitted with dining rooms, galleys, lounges and cabins. They were intended for pleasure cruising on the Nile. Thus even in this respect the kings of Egypt were in advance of kings of industry and European monarchs by several thousand years.

The average length of the Egyptian ships was 100 feet, with a beam of about 20 feet; and they were of 70 to 75 tons burden. Built of timber from Lebanon, they were extremely seaworthy,

22

and their crews safely ventured into the Mediterranean and the Indian Ocean. That they were able to make long sea voyages is not surprising when one considers that voyages of discovery in a much later age were made in ships not much larger than those of the ancient Egyptians: the *Santa Maria* in which Columbus discovered America was of only 100 tons, and his other two ships were of 50 and 40 tons burden, while Magellan's circumnavigation was made with two ships of 110 and 85 tons.

The Egyptians gradually acquired a knowledge of the monsoons and the resulting currents. This enabled them to venture ever farther south down the coast of Africa, to the mouth of the Zambezi and the famed Land of Punt—voyages that they continued to make almost until the end of Egyptian independence. Their ships also made frequent journeys to Phoenician ports, returning with bronze, raw materials necessary for Egyptian manufactures and, especially, ship timber from Lebanon and Syria.

Egypt's relations with eastern Mediterranean ports had existed at a very remote period. There was a legend that went as follows: The god Seth was jealous of Osiris, had him killed and his coffin thrown into the Nile. It drifted out to sea and was eventually washed ashore near Gebal, on the coast of Phoenicia. A large tree sprang up and gathered to it the coffin containing the body of the unfortunate Osiris. His sister Isis, who was seeking everywhere for him, heard about this wonderful tree and went to see it. She sat by a spring where the servants of the Queen of Gebal came every day; she helped them fill their pitchers, and transmitted to their bodies the fragrant odors of her own. Thus did Isis win the heart of the Queen, who made her a present of the wonderful tree enclosing the body of Osiris.

This fine legend probably grew up as a justification of the Egyptian colonization of Gebal (Byblos, a major Phoenician port until the rise of Tyre and Sidon). Legends have often been used to serve political ends. Gebal remained under Egyptian domination for several centuries, until the decline of the empire, when a king of Gebal named Zecher-Baal promptly cast the pharaoh's representatives into a dungeon and had them tortured —unseemly behavior on the part of a descendant of the queen who had been so kind to the Egyptian gods.

The expeditions of the Egyptians, it must be admitted, were not always of an entirely peaceful nature. At a time when Egypt was at the height of her prosperity and power, a military leader realized the important part a fleet could play in a military operation. This was no doubt the first instance of an amphibious

23

operation in the history of mankind, and its planner was none other than Queen Hatshepsut's second husband, Tuthmosis III.

During her reign there had been peace in the empire, and the royal treasuries had acquired a fair amount of wealth. The Queen died when this prosperity was at its height, and apparently without having cultivated the virtues of modesty and simplicity. The temple she had built on the bank of the Nile at Deir el-Bahri, near Thebes, was one of the most splendid of all the Egyptian temples. It was the first monument in antiquity to be given a colonnade—nearly a thousand years before any Greek monument, thus proving that the colonnade was not an innovation of Greek architects, as has long been thought. Deir el-Bahri is a graceful edifice of harmonious proportions. The obelisks found there are the finest as well as the tallest in Egypt. Queen Hatshepsut had many built all over the country, seizing every opportunity to erect one of these eternal witnesses to her greatness and to record for posterity her genius and merits. Her second husband did not seem to have such a high regard for her. Within a short time of her death, Tuthmosis III not only destroyed or effaced images of her and tablets recording her glory, as mentioned earlier, but also effaced the name of her favorite, the high priest Senmut, and those of others who had held important positions at her court. Bitterness, spite and jealousy had caused Tuthmosis to nourish a deep hatred of her. To judge from the great number of reliefs and inscriptions damaged by his orders, Queen Hatshepsut must have been exceedingly generous in distributing privileges and according favored positions. But it must be said in defense of this woman, who was undoubtedly a great sovereign, that unlike many pharaohs she never had her enemies tortured or put to death. And she eventually had the better of Tuthmosis III, for many of her reliefs and inscriptions escaped damage or destruction. When he had two obelisks in the temple at Karnak bricked up he could never have thought that one day, thousands of years later, the screen of bricks would collapse and reveal to the world the record of Queen Hatshepsut's great accomplishments. Over the ages, this stubborn and determined woman still defies Tuthmosis III.

Satisfied at having effaced his wife's memory forever, Tuthmosis III turned his energies to other matters. His ambition was to win a world empire. He had the means and the capabilities, a logical and methodical mind and a sense of strategy worthy of a Napoleon. He believed that a long period of peace (there had been no wars during his wife's reign) could be

24

Tuthmosis III

dangerous for a country, for once the people forgot how to fight, they became an easy prey to their neighbors.

Tuthmosis organized and equipped a large army and first made war on Syria, with the object of obtaining control of the coast. Altogether, he sent four expeditions overland. Each marched out of Egypt as spring was ending and returned in the autumn, having destroyed towns, populations and harvests in the "conquered" country. The first army fought a great battle at Megiddo, in Palestine, which has remained celebrated in the history of the Near East. The Egyptians also measured their might against the forces of Kadesh, Mitani, Byblos, Arvad, and other Canaan city-states which had united in an effort to check the enemy advance. The battle of Megiddo was in fact the first of many, but this was in accordance with the strategic plans of Tuthmosis.

From that time forth, the fortified town of Megiddo at the entrance to the Jezreal valley has often been the scene of battles, right up to the First World War. The geographic situation of Palestine has made her the cockpit of opposing armies and brought her much misery over the centuries.

25

After his fourth expedition, Tuthmosis extended his incursions and imposed his rule over Kadesh and Mitani, whose territories stretched northward into what is now Turkey.

Tuthmosis was renowned for his bravery. Even as an old man, he led his army into battle, thus arousing the admiration of his soldiers. Personal courage was obviously not enough to win an empire, but Tuthmosis was aware of the value of surprise and rapidity of movement in military matters. He began to build a large fleet, and organized another fourteen military expeditions before his death, when the Egyptian dominion to the north included Mesopotamia as well as Palestine and Syria. The fear and terror he inspired among the conquered peoples was such that three generations after his death the mere mention of his name made men tremble.

Tuthmosis used his fleet as troop transports. When the south wind was blowing at the end of spring, he was able to send reinforcements from the Nile Delta to Syria in four or five days. He was the first military leader in history to move his troops by this fast and cheap means. This also enabled him to mount a surprise expedition almost every year. The records speak of him as being "as fleet as the eagle" and "as quick as lightning." The transport of his troops by sea was, however, no easy matter. An Egyptian army of his day numbered twenty-five to thirty thousand. Considering the size of the ships, carrying that number overseas was a triumph of organization. No naval battle was fought—sea warfare would develop much later in history, when ships were better equipped and men had found that it was possible to slaughter enemies not only on dry land.

Tuthmosis III was advanced in years when he died, rich in conquests and satiated with power. He was a great conqueror, a fearless soldier, and the finest military organizer until Alexander the Great. Under Tuthmosis III the Egyptian fleet became a major offensive element in her military strength, because of his having been the first to realize the importance of ships in the conduct of an overseas war.

Philistine prisoners of war;
from temple at Medinet-Abou

Chapter 4

THE PEOPLES OF THE SEA

The greatest pharaoh after Tuthmosis III was Ramses II (thirteenth century B.C.). It was during his reign that the Exodus of the Jews took place.

A tale about Ramses II is recorded on a stone tablet which is now in the Louvre:

In the course of one of his journeys Ramses II arrived at Naharine (Syria), and the ambassadors of various kings and princes came with gifts to pay homage to him, as was befitting a powerful sovereign who dominated the world. Among the delegations was one from Bakhtan (Bactria), which was headed by the king himself. He made Ramses a present of one of his daughters, the most beautiful. (In antiquity, such gifts were often made, leading to alliances and pacts of friendship.) Ramses accepted this gift with great satisfaction.

(The great pharaoh is said to have married five times and to have had one hundred and sixty-two children—a figure difficult to accept, despite the fact that the oriental is known to be prolific in this respect.)

Some time later, an envoy of the King of Bakhtan arrived at the court of Ramses to ask for the services of a physician, as the princess' sister was gravely ill. (The healing arts of the Egyptians had a great reputation all over the ancient world.)

27

Ramses sent his father-in-law one of his most learned physicians, but the therapeutic treatment was of no avail. So another envoy came to ask Ramses to intervene personally, for it was known that the gods have infinite powers. This time Ramses sent the god of destiny, Chonsu, whose power was great. The Egyptians were aware that Destiny (in other words, Nature) could sometimes heal when the best physicians were powerless. They knew that sick people could often cure themselves by sheer will power and that the gods have infinite powers. This was the reason for the god himself—that is to say, his statue—being put by Ramses on a large Egyptian ship, which then set sail for India escorted by five other ships.

This small fleet is said to have reached its destination after a voyage which lasted seventeen months. The ships reached the mouth of the Indus and then sailed up the river to Bakhtan. For three years and nine months the god Chonsu fought against the illness of the young princess, and finally prevailed. The princess recovered her health, and the god of destiny was able to return to Egypt. There, he was given great honor and received many offerings from the pharaoh, nor were those who had accompanied the god forgotten.

The interest to us in this tale—for there are good reasons to believe it to be true—lies in the fact that Egyptian ships made several voyages to Bakhtan and back, a distance of nearly six thousand miles for the round-trip voyage, within a comparatively short period.

Surviving writings give evidence of trade relations between Egypt and India dating back to very early times. This trade was chiefly in precious stones. The many sapphires or lapis lazuli that have been found all over Egypt, in the decoration of statues, encrusted in furniture or mounted as jewelry, came exclusively from India. The trade in precious stones was always most flourishing—the ancients were quite as keen speculators as the moderns—and it is not surprising that there should have been almost regular sea communications between Egypt and India from a quite early period.

Ramses II was known as "the Great," and he certainly had a great family—his children and grandchildren were so numerous that they formed a distinct aristocratic clan. He was pharaoh for sixty-seven years, one of the longest reigns in history. It is particularly outstanding since he did not succeed to the throne until he was twenty-three.

Toward the end of his reign the decline of the empire began. Egypt was gravely threatened by invaders who united against

28

a country showing signs of weariness and ruled by an old man well past his prime. These invaders, whom the Egyptians called "the Peoples of the Sea," were halted only at the frontiers. Who were they? The Egyptians gave the name of Peoples of the Sea to all the tribes of the north. By the twelfth century B.C. there was a great amalgamation of peoples in the eastern Mediterranean, chiefly nomadic tribes who had moved south, pillaging and destroying as they went. Some are known to us, but many are lost to history. The Philistines were probably one of these Peoples of the Sea, having established themselves in southern Palestine after the devastations on Crete.

The "Denyens," whose name appears in writings of the period, have been identified by some historians as the Danaoi, a general term for the early settlers in Greece. "Cheklesh" and "Chereden" may have been names for the inhabitants of Sicily and Sardinia, while the "Ekwech" are believed to have been Achaeans. But none of these names seems to have any linguistic association. And who were the "Terech"? On the other hand, the Peoples of the Sea included the Hittites, the Lydians, and other tribes of Asia Minor whose names have a place in history.

At the same time as these peoples from the north were threatening Egypt, nomadic tribes from Libya were invading the Delta, driven by hunger and privations. An inscription made during the reign of Merenptah, successor to Ramses II, records that these tribes "constantly overrun the country and wage war in order to fill their bellies." There was, in fact, a great famine in all the lands at that time. The migration of the tribes of

The Ship of the Gods

Israel, as recorded in the Book of Genesis, was but part of a general movement in search of food, a movement from all directions upon a single goal—Egypt.

Merenptah was advanced in years when he succeeded his father. He had been thirteenth in the line of succession, but Ramses the Great had lived so long that twelve of the heirs to the throne had predeceased him.

Egypt's heyday was past, and Merenptah found himself constantly on the defense against the invaders. The bas-reliefs and inscriptions of his day tell of his struggles and his triumphs, and hymns of praise and gratitude abound on pillars, for he had "crushed the enemy, and none of the nine peoples of the bow raises their head." But such flattery bore little relation to the real facts of the situation.

However many victories the chroniclers attributed to Merenptah, they did not prevent conditions in Egypt from worsening steadily. There was complete disorder in the country for fifteen years after his death, until the accession of Ramses III in 1198 B.C. He was young and energetic. Considered to be the founder of the twentieth dynasty, he was perhaps the last great pharaoh.

The Peoples of the Sea had allied themselves with the King of Libya, and the combined forces were making a vigorous attack on the Delta by land and sea. Ramses III marched to meet them, and won a great battle near a fortress called Aroukh— a victory long renowned in Egyptian history. The large fleet of the Peoples of the Sea was almost completely destroyed. The few ships that succeeded in putting to sea were overhauled by the Egyptians, who killed a large number of their enemies. Twelve thousand, according to the chroniclers, were killed in the battle, and a thousand were taken into captivity.

Ramses showed great courage during the fighting, "attacking hundreds of thousands of the enemy . . . no warrior in the world was his equal at drawing the bow to such effect. . . ." These official praises were naturally a little overdone; the scribes were good enough courtiers not to fail to exaggerate the merits of their king. So all epic descriptions, and even ordinary records of the reign of Ramses III, should be treated with some reserve, in particular when it is said that the situation in Egypt had improved so much that women were again able to go about without wearing a veil. For the pharaoh was soon obliged to admit that even veils were no longer sufficient protection for Egyptian women. The Peoples of the Sea, by no means deterred by their defeat, were returning to the attack. With their allies,

30

The first known picture of a
naval battle, showing Ramses III
triumphing over the
Peoples of the Sea

the Philistines and the Libyans, they were approaching the
Delta again, having devastated a few small kingdoms—such
as that of the Hittites—in their progress. Ramses III suddenly
became aware of the grave danger to his country. He
strengthened the defenses on the Syrian frontier, then raised an
army of foot soldiers and cavalry, and built a large fleet that was
sent to defend the Syrian ports where the people, the Phoenicians, were loyal to Egypt. The pharaoh recorded that, because
of his actions, "the ports were defended by warships manned by
rowers and by a vast number of craft that formed a strong
rampart. There were brave warriors shouting defiance on the
prow and stern of the ships, like lions roaring on the summit of
mountains."

Ramses went to Syria to take command of his troops. With
"much modesty" he recorded for future generations: "I have been

31

Munt the strong, the god of war; I camped before them so that all could grasp my hands, the hands of the King of Upper and Lower Egypt, who chastised Hatamcho [the Libyans, probably a reference to his first victory over them], the hands of the son of Ramses-Ra, the all-powerful prince. I bore myself as a bold leader who knows the strength of his arm, whose influence is felt afar and who assists his soldiers on the day of battle." This gives much insight into the pharaoh's character. After this, it is not surprising that the Egyptian army under the command of a god named Ramses won the day!

There were in fact two battles, one on land and the other at sea. The name of the place where the former took place is not known to us, but it was a great victory for Ramses. . . . All the happenings of his reign are recorded on the walls of the temple he built west of Thebes in honor of the god Amon. He was always enlarging this temple and making it more beautiful, adding annexes and covering the walls with inscriptions and reliefs, so that they provide a complete record, a chronicle of the achievements of Ramses III. Nowhere is there anything to compare with the verbiage of these inscriptions and their pompous style, even in the annals of ancient Egypt.

The pharaoh's army is shown on the reliefs breaking the enemy ranks, putting them to flight, and leading into captivity the women and children of the Peoples of the Sea—taking them in chariots drawn by bullocks.

When the land battle was won, Ramses hurried to the support of his navy. He posted groups of archers in the ships, and their arrows created havoc among the enemy before he could get near enough to board. Egyptian archers were also drawn up on the shore as "artillery support," and their "fire" added to the destruction in the enemy ships. Then the Egyptian ships advanced to the attack.

The heavy losses already suffered by the Peoples of the Sea had caused fear and confusion among them, and this developed into outright panic when the Egyptians boarded their ships. "They were slaughtered, and their bodies piled up in their boats from stem to stern, and then they were thrown into the sea." Some escaped and succeeded in swimming ashore, only to be killed by the Egyptian soldiers.

In this manner do the inscriptions on the temple of Amon describe the first naval battle in history. But even more interesting are the reliefs showing the Egyptian warships attacking and their archers sending a shower of arrows into the enemy ships, which can be distinctly seen. Here for the first

32

PLATE 2

Egyptian ship of about the eighteenth century B.C.

This is a model designed by Dr. Sotas and built by M. I. Krupnik from very ancient drawings preserved in the tombs of Aboukir and dating from the reign of the Pharaoh Sahouré. The fleet of this pharaoh sailed along the coast of Phoenicia, bringing back cedarwood and Semitic slaves. The ship shown here has no wooden keel, the function of a spine being performed by an elastic cable under maximum tension. It was twisted by means of a bar inserted between the strands. The structure was reinforced by means of beams in the hold which served as stiffeners. Although the hull is wooden, it still bears some resemblance in outline to the Nile boats with wickerwork frames. This boat is with a square-rigged sail narrow in proportion to its height, on an inverted V-shaped mast, and propelled by eight oars on a side. There are six more steering oars, three on either side.

The master and the pilot took post on the poop. Sailors and soldiers slept on deck, where cargo also was stored. The eye painted on the prow is very frequently found in ancient ships, and, indeed, on some Mediterranean boats today, as well as further afield on Malayan sampans, Chinese junks and Arab dhows.

PLATE 2

Egyptian ship of about the eighteenth century B.C.

time are the Peoples of the Sea portrayed in stone by their contemporaries. We can see what they looked like, how they were dressed and what weapons they used.

Ramses' victories saved Egypt from invasion and at last tempered the ardor of the Peoples of the Sea. But Egypt was not left in peace for long. The next enemy came from the west. A people called the Mechwech (about whom very little is known) invaded the Delta, and Ramses again gathered together his army to repulse them. "He fell upon them like a mountain of granite," the chroniclers recorded for posterity. "They were utterly crushed and their blood flowed in streams. Their bodies were mutilated and trodden into the ground...." And peace again came to Egypt.

Ramses was then able to devote himself to the building of magnificent temples to the glory of the gods, and of monuments worthy of his name and glorious reign. He sent a large expedition to Punt to obtain choice offerings particularly appreciated by the gods. The priests of Egypt had more riches heaped upon them than ever before in the history of the country.

It was not long, however, before the peoples on the frontiers of the empire rose against their masters once more. The Phoenicians and the city-states in southern Palestine, and those in Libya, threw off the Egyptian yoke. The death of Ramses III in 1167 B.C. marked the end of the military pharaohs. The decline of Egypt's political power had definitely set in.

**Detail of naval battle
of Ramses III**

Chapter 5

A CANAL LINKING TWO SEAS

The history of the Suez Canal goes back very much earlier than the mid-nineteenth century. As we have already seen, Egyptian ships were able to pass from the Nile to the Red Sea by way of a canal in the time of Queen Hatshepsut. And the idea of the canal was even older. After all, considering the geographical position of Egypt, her rulers were bound to think of a means to facilitate communications between the Red Sea and the Mediterranean that would reduce the cost of transport and aid military expeditions. Besides, having engaged in irrigation works since time immemorial, the ancient Egyptians were specialists in the making of canals. Their network of irrigation canals was of a high quality and included reservoirs and artificial lakes. As canals could be dug to irrigate the fields, there seemed no reason why others should not be dug for boats to pass along.

The first attempts were made near the first cataract, which was called "The Door of the South." This door had for long been the route by which Nubian tribes invaded Egypt. They suddenly appeared out of the desert, pillaged and destroyed villages, then disappeared back into the desert as quickly as they had come. Pursuit of them was difficult because land operations required lengthy preparation.

Pepi I, a powerful pharaoh who reigned in the twenty-sixth century B.C., gave orders for five canals to be dug in the granite

35

**The Pharaoh Tarhaka captured by
the King of Assyria, Assarhadon**

rock to bypass the first cataract. Work went on for more than
a year, by which time there was a continuous waterway enabling
the Egyptian army to reach the heart of the region peopled by
the Nubian tribes, who were soon subdued. The canals were also
used to bring down blocks of stone and granite for the
construction of the splendid monuments. If it had not been for
the initiative of the early pharaohs, the great obelisks and their
inscriptions recording the kings' exploits might never have
existed.

The work begun by Pepi I was continued by later pharaohs.
Surviving documents prove that other navigation canals were
made. During the reign of Senusert III, who seems to have had
a highly developed technical mind, the canals made around the
first cataract by Pepi I were deepened and widened. One was
a hundred yards long, thirty-three feet wide and thirty feet
deep, and could take the largest boats of the time. Documentary
evidence also points to the existence at that time of the canal
linking the Nile with the Red Sea. It went from the most eastern
arm of the Nile—of the seven then forming the Delta—along
the Wadi Tamilat and into Lake Amer, and then from the lake
to the head of the Red Sea.

The towns in the Delta were meeting places for all manner
of people come from afar to sell their merchandise to the wealthy
Egyptians. The area was a permanent exchange mart for the
products of the East and the West; shells were sold for amber,

panther skins from Africa for bronze articles from Tarsus or Gades (Cadiz).

In those times Egypt was a center of international trade, and her pharaohs realized that the canal was the best guarantee of a continuance of power and wealth. It constituted, for Egypt, an ever-open door to the East; and for Africa and India a direct link with the countries of the West. Ramses II had every reason for protecting the routes to Suez. The Delta town of Pitom, where the harvests were stored and stocks of amber and other riches were kept, was also a military base and fortress, strategically placed to defend the sea routes. Even the town of Per-Ramses ("the house of Ramses") was built in the Delta. The great pharaoh intended it to be his capital, the chief warehouse of the royal treasuries.

As we read in the Bible, Ramses the Great forced the children of Israel to work on the building of these towns, and applied cruel measures. Most of the great building projects of the distant past were, alas, carried out with the tears, sweat and blood of subject peoples.

The canal often became unusable because of obstruction from silt and drifting sand, but several pharaohs had the imagination and foresight to order the canal to be cleared out. Its fate depended, nevertheless, on the interest taken in it by the reigning king. The reverses of fortune that occur in the history of peoples and empires were also the lot of the canal. In spite of the great benefit it had been, it was finally abandoned when Egypt's decline set in.

Six centuries after Ramses the Great, the country was roused from its long torpor. Native Saite rulers attempted to restore her greatness. Psammetichus I and his son Necho II, in particular, made great efforts to revive Egyptian prestige. Necho (610–594 B.C.) sent trade missions to distant lands, chartered ships and fitted out a fleet. These activities naturally led to fresh interest in the canal, and Necho ordered work to be started on digging a new bed.

Herodotus, who traveled in Egypt one hundred and thirty years after the death of Necho, wrote about the canal:

> Necho, son of Psammetichus, began constructing the canal which stretches from the Nile to the Arabian Gulf, and it was later completed by Darius the Persian. The length of the canal is four days' journey by boat. It is wide enough to allow two boats each with three pairs

of rowers to proceed abreast. The water in the canal is that of the Nile. It leaves the river just south of Bubastis, not far from Patumus, an Arabian town, and passes across the Egyptian plain on the Arabian side, a little north of the chain of hills as far as Memphis, where the stone quarries are found; it curves round these hills, from the west to the east, then passes through a narrow gorge; after that, it takes a southerly direction and ends in the Arabian Gulf [Red Sea]. The shortest distance from the Mediterranean, or North Sea, to the South Sea, or Indian Ocean, that is to say from Mount Cassius, between Egypt and Syria, to the Arabian Gulf, is about 150 miles. That is the most direct way; but by the canal, which by no means follows a straight line, the journey is much longer. The construction of the canal in the time of King Necho cost the lives of 120,000 Egyptians. Necho did not complete the work. He broke it off because an oracle warned him that the canal would only benefit the "barbarians," as the Egyptians called all those who did not speak their language.

Herodotus often interlarded his descriptions with legends and popular tales he picked up during his travels, and his remarks are spiced with a bantering humor to be expected from a writer who is aware that his knowledge adds to the wisdom of his contemporaries. His estimate of distances and his geographical indications are far from being exact; he had no means of measuring, and trusted what others had said and written before him. This explains the little error in the distance from the Mediterranean to the Red Sea. On the other hand, his figure of 120,000 who died in digging the canal is quite conceivable. The hygienic and working conditions then prevailing were far worse than in the time of De Lesseps; and as thousands of Egyptian fellahin succumbed to conditions in the nineteenth century while helping to build the Suez Canal, it could hardly be an exaggeration to estimate that over a hundred thousand slaves were killed off doing a similar task twenty-five centuries previously.

It is difficult to judge whether Necho did not complete the canal for the reason given by Herodotus or through some other cause. Even if the figure of 120,000 fatalities is considered doubtful, the fact remains that tens of thousands of laborers must still have been digging the canal. Necho met with several military defeats and was obliged to restrain his enthusiasm for

38

Sketch map of ancient Egypt

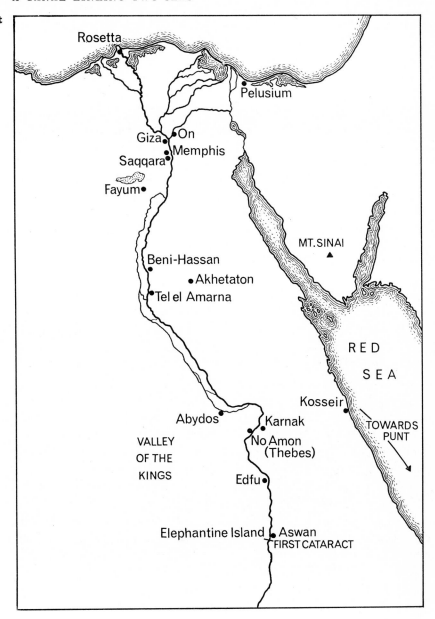

construction projects. The royal treasury was being emptied at an alarming rate, and the pharaoh had to stop the work into which he had already poured huge sums of money and a great many human lives. The decision was, of course, attributed to the gods. Men have always been credulous enough to accept divine decisions without question. In fact it would appear that public opinion already existed in the time of the last pharaohs.

Several of the later conquerors and rulers of Egypt continued the work on the canal begun by Necho. The commercial and strategic advantages to be obtained from it were apparent throughout the centuries, from antiquity to medieval times. Diodorus, the Greek historian who visited Egypt at the beginning of the Christian era, wrote: "They have dug a canal from the Pelusium arm [one of the seven arms of the Nile] to the Red Sea. Necho had begun it; Darius, King of the Persians, continued it; and Ptolemy II completed it. He had locks made at appropriate points along the canal. These are opened for boats to enter the canal and are closed again immediately afterward."

Darius is known to have made use of the canal for his military expeditions, notably when he sent a fleet to attack the Greeks. The description given by Diodorus points to the canals having been a vital artery of communication in the time of Ptolemy II, and even for another two hundred years. But the locks he mentioned were probably no more than gates to control the passage of boats and, especially, the payment of taxes and duty on their cargoes.

At the battle of Actium in 31 B.C. Cleopatra saw that Anthony had lost the day and she fled from the scene with her warships, and tried to get through the canal. Her attempt failed, because years of neglect had left it obstructed in several places.

The emperor Trajan, who greatly developed the road communications of the Roman empire, had the canal cleaned out again and brought back into use. The historians of his time had every reason for naming it "Trajan's canal." Work on it continued during the reign of his successor, Hadrian.

The centuries passed. With the spread of Christianity came pilgrimages to the Holy Land. In the fifth and sixth centuries A.D. there was an almost constant flow of pilgrims—a contact between Europe and the Near East that, a few centuries later, resulted in the Crusades. Some of these early pilgrims wrote accounts of their travels, and those which have survived give a good idea of geographical knowledge in the early Middle Ages.

In the latter part of the sixth century an inhabitant of Piacenza named Antoninus wrote a detailed account of his journey to Palestine and beyond. It contains a large number of improbable stories that reflect the superstitious beliefs of the time. Nevertheless, a modern authority on medieval geography, C. R. Beazley, believes there is a certain amount of reliability in some of the account.

The "marvels and wonders" described by Antoninus can obviously be disregarded. He writes of Abyssinians without nose or ears—mutilations supposedly made by order of the emperor

40

Trajan to distinguish this race from others. Antoninus was also impressed by the great white statue of Baal on Mount Sinai, which apparently changed color in the moonlight and at the sight of a pagan began to tremble and became as black as tar. Wonders of this kind were accepted as facts in early medieval times. Yet elements of truth are contained among all the fiction. Antoninus writes of visiting Eilath, "a trading center for India and the Red Sea where the traveler can see ships loaded with spices of all kinds." He went on to Clysma (Suez) by way of the canal, and saw ships from India anchored there. This was the place, he explains, where the children of Israel crossed the Red Sea. At low tide the debris of Pharaoh's army and the tracks made by his war chariots could still be seen . . . All the weapons of the Egyptian army had been turned into marble. At Suez he ate green hazelnuts, which came from India, but which many people said had come originally from the Garden of Eden . . . And the good pilgrim produces one marvelous story after another. But the really interesting fact among it all is that in his day the famous canal still existed and was in use.

Egypt knew many foreign rulers. The Ptolemies were replaced by Roman emperors, and then the Arabs. In the middle of the seventh century the Caliph Omar had the canal cleaned out and made fit for navigation once again. His reasons were largely strategic, to speed communications between Arabia and occupied Egypt, though there were economic as well as military needs to be considered.

In the early Middle Ages the Irish were great travelers. Some were missionaries and among them were real scholars. Dicuilus, an Irish historian and one of the most learned of his time, wrote a book in 825 entitled *Extent of the Terrestrial Globe*. It was an attempt to bring together all the geographical knowledge of his age, and included an account of a pilgrimage to the Holy Land made by an Irish monk named Fidelis sometime during the decade 750–760. This pilgrimage followed a roundabout route, as Fidelis sailed up the Nile to the Red Sea. Dicuilus gave much attention to this journey, to demonstrate that one arm of the Nile flowed into the Red Sea. He was probably unaware that the waterway used by his compatriot was the canal dug during the reign of Necho and subsequently put to use by the conquerors of Egypt: the Persians, Greeks, Romans, and Arabs. It was not until 767 that the Caliph of Baghdad gave orders for the canal to be filled in, to hinder attacks by Muslims who had remained in the Arabian peninsula. The account given by

41

Dicuilus can therefore be treated with all seriousness. The reports he made of Fidelis' journeys appear more truthful than most of the descriptions given by medieval travelers. Fidelis spoke only of what he had seen with his own eyes, and was cautious about the conclusions he drew for his contemporaries.

Then the canal fell into disuse. The spread of the Muslim empire caused it to be abandoned. Wind and weather completed the destruction of the waterway that for so many centuries had linked two seas. But signs of it remained visible for many centuries still; mention of them is found in accounts of travelers throughout the Middle Ages and up to Renaissance times.

Ancient Egyptian ship

Chapter 6

THE VOYAGE AROUND AFRICA

Egypt was often invaded in the course of her long history, but she always absorbed and assimilated her conquerors. Then the rapid rise of Assyria made a clash with Egypt inevitable. She still enjoyed great prestige, although weak and in decline, and her legendary riches amassed over the centuries aroused great jealousy.

The result of the clash between Assyria and Egypt was not difficult to foresee. Had not the prophet Isaiah (whose political sense was acute) already compared Egypt to a broken reed?

"Neither shall there be any work for Egypt, which the head or tail, branch or rush, may do.

"In that day shall Egypt be like unto women: and it shall be afraid and fear because of the shaking of the hand of the Lord of Hosts, which he shaketh over it." (xix, 15 & 16.)

Thus had the prophet written of the weak state and decline of Egypt. His penetrating mind had correctly appraised the situation and drawn the conclusion:

"And the Lord said, Like as my servant Isaiah hath walked naked and barefoot three years, for a sign and wonder upon Egypt and upon Ethiopia.

"So shall the king of Assyria lead away the Egyptians prisoners, and the Ethiopians captives, young and old, naked and barefoot, even with their buttocks uncovered, to the shame of Egypt." (xx, 3 & 4.)

The prophet Isaiah saw clearly, but the kings of Israel and of Aram-Naharayim paid no attention to his warnings. They took a different view of the prevailing situation; there were no doubt numbers of Egyptian envoys in the Near East, distributing presents and making promises in order to obtain allies against the might of Assyria. This policy succeeded for a time. The Egyptians raised a protective barrier between themselves and the Assyrians, which broke the first assaults of the latter. But pressure continued, and finally Sennacherib crushed all resistance and marched into Egypt, which fell into his hands like a ripe fruit.

The Assyrians imposed heavy taxes on the country, accumulated booty and generally showed who was master. Their yoke, however, did not weigh too heavily on the conquered people; administration of the country was left in Egyptian hands. As often happens in a period of national decadence, the people turned to their brilliant past and there was a renaissance of Egyptian culture. From the Delta town of Sais came princes to lead a national revival. These Saite rulers, Psammetichus I and his son Necho, were clever, realistic politicians and excellent organizers. Moreover, they realized that the Egyptian peoples

Map of Africa
as seen by a German
geographer of the
sixteenth century

were past their heyday and had lost their combative spirit, and so mercenaries were needed in order to wage war. These were recruited from Greece, Asia Minor, and other areas of the Near East, and the army thus assembled gave Egypt a brief impression of having recovered her greatness. In addition to organizing military forces the Saite rulers developed the country's trade and endeavored to raise the standards of living. All this was most necessary if the country was to support the burden of a standing army of mercenaries. Greek traders were allowed to settle in the Delta, and Greek and Phoenician ships sailed freely on the Nile. The resulting commercial benefits, a sounder economy, soon enabled Egypt to dream of conquest again.

The Assyrians were beginning to show signs of exhaustion too.... It was in this political climate that Psammetichus—and more so his son—planned greater expansion and even began to put their projects into effect. Necho devoted great energy to having the canal dug, and he appointed commissions to seek out new openings for trade along distant shores. Probably his most ambitious sea expedition was the voyage around Africa, though the crews were admittedly not Egyptian but Phoenician, and the ships were chartered. The credit nevertheless belongs to the Egyptian rulers, whose last major enterprise it was. They supplied the initiative and the money, and this attempt to circumnavigate the African continent fitted in with the rest of Necho's plans.

The main source of information about this voyage is Herodotus, who wrote:

> Libya [that is, Africa] shows that it has sea all round except the part that borders on Asia, Necho a king of Egypt being the first within our knowledge to show this fact; for when he stopped digging the canal which stretches from the Nile to the Arabian Gulf he sent forth Phoenician men in ships, ordering them to sail back between the Pillars of Hercules until they came to the Northern [Mediterranean] Sea and thus to Egypt. The Phoenicians therefore setting forth from the Red Sea sailed in the Southern Sea [Arabian Sea and Indian Ocean], and whenever autumn came they each time put ashore and sowed the land wherever they might be in Libya as they voyaged, and awaited the reaping time; having then reaped the corn they set sail, so that after the passing of two years they doubled the Pillars of Hercules in the third year and came to Egypt. And they told things believable perhaps for others but unbeliev-

able for me, namely that in sailing round Libya they had the sun on the right hand. Thus was Libya known for the first time.

That is the plain bald statement, dry and disappointing, lacking in the travelers' tales and descriptions usually given by Herodotus. But its essentials have caused every sort of comment over a period of 2,400 years.

Did the expedition really take place? And if so, who were Herodotus' informants? (He was writing about one hundred and fifty years after the alleged voyage.) So many questions spring to mind on reading this astonishing account. Numerous books and papers have been written about it, and experts have taken decidedly opposed positions about it.

Yet there is no doubt that Herodotus wrote that passage after hearing about the voyage from Egyptian priests or Phoenician sailors during his stay in Egypt. Although he casts doubts on it himself, his account contains a geographical fact which he entirely accepted—that Africa has "sea all round it except the part that borders on Asia."

The ancients were well aware of it, but over the centuries the knowledge was forgotten. Only three centuries after Herodotus, we find Ptolemy the geographer giving the Indian Ocean as an enclosed sea and maintaining that South Africa was joined to the Asiatic continent. It may have been partly the fault of Herodotus. The doubts he cast on the authenticity of the expedition were perhaps mistakenly taken as applying to all the information in the account.

But let us examine the possibilities of the circumnavigation of Africa by the Phoenicians. The distance would be about 14,000 miles, which seems a fantastic voyage for the times, because of the sort of ships then built and the lack of navigational aids such as the mariner's compass. Yet Egyptian and Phoenician ships were quite seaworthy, and instances taken from the Middle Ages show that very long voyages were not impossible in smallish ships. In 1539 the Portuguese Diego Botelho sailed safely from Goa to Lisbon in a boat sixteen feet long and nine broad!

In my opinion there can be no doubt as to the authenticity of the expedition.

The principal argument on which Herodotus based his disbelief in the voyage can easily be refuted. The story of the sun's appearing on the right hand of the voyagers seemed to him an obvious fairy tale. But it should not be held against Herodotus that he was ignorant of a patent fact known to all who sailed

Pottery painting, showing ancient Cretan sailing ship

down the coast of Africa. Herodotus was a man of the northern hemisphere, to whom such a thing seemed so absurd that he hesitated to include it in his account. Fortunately for posterity the journalist in him prevailed over the geographer and historian. The disbelief in the sun's appearing on the right (that is, to the north of their ships, instead of being in the south, at midday) may well have been the reason, as much as the perpetuating of the idea that southern Africa was joined to India, why no further attempts were made to circumnavigate Africa until Vasco da Gama and the Portuguese explorers of the fifteenth century.

As for making a voyage of 14,000 miles without the aid of the compass, the Phoenicians of Necho's time knew all about the monsoons and the currents of the Indian Ocean. The Egyptians had long been making voyages to India, the Land of Punt, Ceylon and even China. Moreover, when the sailors of those days ventured into unknown waters they kept within sight of the coast; and the coast of Africa would be an excellent "compass" for the circumnavigation.

The crews needed to be men of great physical and moral courage. They were going into the unknown, to land on mysterious shores where all manner of dangers lurked. But the

47

Phoenicians were fearless and bold sailors, and they had no idea of the kind of perils ahead of them. It is knowledge that creates fear.

Objections have been raised that the crews could not have withstood the privations of a voyage lasting three years. How did they obtain their food and water? They knew nothing of methods of preserving food, and their ships were too small to allow enough fresh water for such a long voyage to be carried. But they were used to the simplest of diets. The Mediterranean peoples were practically vegetarians in those days, and could go without meat for months on end. The basic daily ration of a Roman soldier, for instance, was two pounds of flour. He was also issued some olive oil and honey, both of which keep a long time.

The ships remained within sight of the coast as much as possible, and so the crews could put in to seek fresh fruit and vegetables when their stores were getting low. This was not without its dangers, for they would not always be welcomed by the natives. They often had to fight to get a little food—and, unlike later explorers, they had no firearms. Gunpowder had not then been invented, or, if the Chinese were indeed already using it, their knowledge had not spread to the Mediterranean peoples.

In Necho's time, ships leaving on long voyages carried supplies of grain (of quick-growing kinds), and at the right season the crews landed and grew corn, reaped the harvest and then set sail again.

During the time ashore the sailors would explore the hinterland, and obtain local produce from the natives, by force if necessary. The risks and perils of the voyage were many, and hunger and suffering must have added to the tribulations of the travelers. Many undoubtedly died on the way. There were the various diseases, scurvy in particular, resulting from insufficient food and an unbalanced diet, as well as the sufferings due to prolonged periods ashore in unhealthy tropical climates.

But the dangers from hostile tribes, malnutrition, and disease were not the worst. The greatest sufferings of the crews came from lack of fresh water. The usual practice of sailors in those days was to take a supply of drinking water in large earthenware jars; but they were heavy and took up much space, so not many could be carried in the small ships. This problem remained a crucial one for deep-sea sailors for many centuries—even keeping water in large casks did not much improve matters—and was still a major anxiety in the seventeenth century.

PLATE 3

Egyptian ship of the fifteenth century B.C., reign of Hatshepsut

This type of ship has been reconstructed to a design by M. Pliner, a naval architect, and built by M. I. Krupnik of the Haifa Maritime Museum, on the basis of a wall painting in the temple at Deir el-Bahri. It represents in low relief a fleet of five ships fitting out for a trading voyage on the orders of Queen Hatshepsut.

The dimensions were 21 or 22 meters long by 5½ wide, the hull being 1½ meters deep and massively built. The prow is curved and ornamented with a lotus-flower figurehead. Here the keel is replaced by the elastic spine of thick rope. This is one effect of the lack of large building timbers in Egypt. The spine cable was stretched along the longitudinal axis of the ship, over supporting pillars and between undergirths at bow and stern. The ship carried 30 oars, 15 each side, and there was a very wide square sail. The mast is here cut out of one piece. The rudder is a double steering oar, with two handles for the use of the pilot. Compared with earlier examples, the construction of this vessel shows appreciable progress in design.

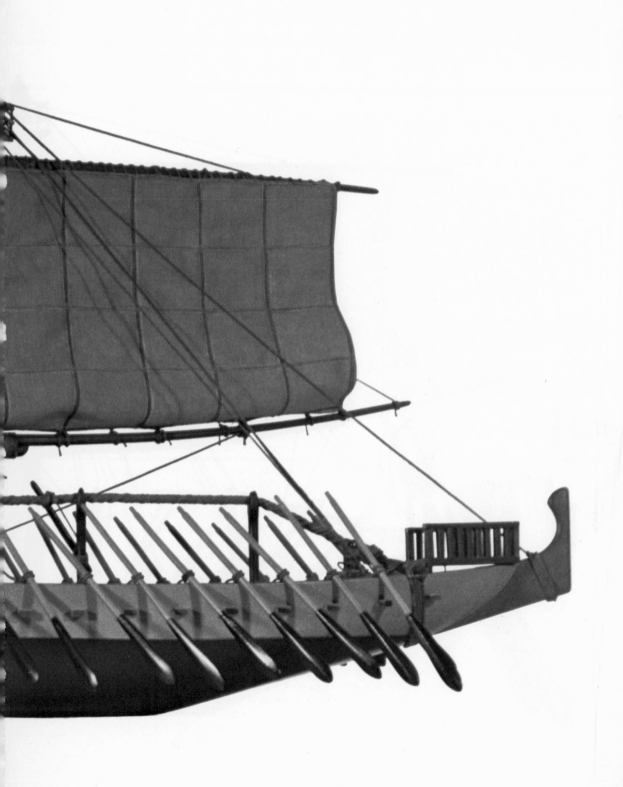

PLATE 3

Egyptian ship of the fifteenth century B.C.

The ancients apparently knew that in extremity some relief could be obtained by boiling sea water and collecting the condensation. The use of this method by sailors was mentioned by St. Basil, who lived in the latter part of the fourth century A.D., at Cesarea, a Palestine port. But although the method might save a man's life, it did not solve the problem of thirst. What were the motives, one wonders, that led the ancients to make long and difficult sea expeditions? They were first and foremost a quest for new wealth—for gold, rather than a desire for fresh knowledge. The voyagers, unlike modern explorers, had no scientific preoccupations. Even a religious urge, a desire to spread the faith, was lacking in the ancients. They were probably just as much possessed by the demon of curiosity, but it was not merely curiosity which drove the Greeks to set forth. And the Romans penetrated to unknown lands because of an urge for conquest. The determining factor in all these expeditions was always, in fact, a craving for wealth and gain. Gold drew men on, as did trade and spices. In antiquity, the object of major expeditions was strictly materialistic. Necho conceived the idea of digging the canal, but there were solid commercial reasons behind this bold enterprise. He was beaten in battle by the Assyrians, and the eastern Mediterranean shores came under their domination, but trade with the peoples of the north and the west was not affected. Necho was unable to complete the canal, and so he sought other possibilities of extending trade. He believed the African continent could be sailed around, and he drew the logical conclusion. The discovery of new sea routes had become imperative. Ships laden with the produce of Arabia, India, Persia, and Ethiopia had to be able to reach the markets of the north without coming under the control of the Assyrians. Much was at stake. Necho had all the qualities for organizing such a daring expedition, and the Phoenician sailors had all the skills needed for its success. The latter were known to be fearless, and their powers of endurance were proverbial. They knew the sea and its ways, and loved it. They lived on it and drew their living from it. Necho had the money, and the Phoenicians were always attracted by that. The pharaoh must have promised them great commercial advantages as well as paying them well.

All these factors tend to show that the doubts expressed by Herodotus were without justification. The sceptics (they will always be with us!) have pointed out that no record of the voyage has ever been found in the Egyptian "archives"; and it is strange that neither the Egyptians nor the Phoenicians ever repeated the voyage (supposing it did take place), and even stranger that no travelers' tales, descriptions of wild tribes and so on, were handed down—the kind of details which the Phoenicians and the Greeks, with their avid taste for epic literature, would have been bound to retain.

But why should the Phoenicians have repeated a voyage that had brought no commercial gain? They were men of action and realists in matters of business. The expedition had been exceedingly costly and dangerous, and had brought no profit or advantage. This is also the explanation for the Phoenicians' not making a detailed report. Frightening stories of horrible monsters and yawning chasms were told by the Greeks and the Phoenicians with the sole object of deterring trade competitors from following them to new and profitable markets.

It is possible that a report was made to the Egyptians, but this was kept a state secret. Even in Renaissance times, information about sea routes was jealously guarded by the state. It may be that the returning Phoenicians had no desire to publish details about the regions beyond the Straits of Gibraltar. The Atlantic (the coast of Spain and of Morocco) was, so to speak, a monopoly of the Phoenicians.

None of the objections, it can be seen, is without an answer. The fact remains that Phoenicians were sent out by Necho and sailed around Africa from the Red Sea to the Mediterranean. A German, W. Müller, many years ago published a book, *Die Umsegelung Afrikas*, in which he gave a detailed description of how the expedition could have performed its task: the time of year it set out, how it could have been helped by the winds and the currents, when and where the crews landed to sow wheat, and when they set sail again. No doubt the author drew on his imagination, but his scheme fits and demonstrates that Necho's expedition sailed down the east coast of Africa, saw the sun rise on the right hand, and reached the Mediterranean from the Atlantic.

The circumnavigation of Africa by Necho's expedition was one of the most amazing achievements in the history of mankind. The voyage of Magellan in the sixteenth century was wonderful enough; how much more so, then, was that of the Phoenicians in the sixth century B.C.

There was a brief revival of Egyptian splendor and culture under Psammetichus and Necho. This last glow flared into a great flame before dying away completely. Yet, although there was still some warmth in the flame, it could shed but a dim light over the historical background of the country. The sun which had shone so proudly in the Egyptian firmament for

50

several millennia was sinking wearily to its western rest. Necho's efforts were a final attempt at restoring the power, the glory and the culture of Egypt. When his dynasty fell, the peoples and city-states, still believing that the Egyptian scepter was unbroken, fell with it. Assyria went under to Babylonia. Then the Medes, and after them the Persians, conquered Babylonia. Egypt fell into the hands of these new masters, becoming one of the richest satrapies in the empire of Cambyses, King of Persia.

More than two thousand years had passed since the building of the Great Pyramids, and the words of the prophet Ezekiel— "And there shall be no more a prince of the land of Egypt"— came true; as did the forebodings of a son of Egypt in her decline: "Woe to thee, O Egypt, thy religion has become a legend, and thy children no longer believe in it. All that shall remain of thee are words engraved on stone, telling of thy past greatness." And of all her splendid past there now remain only hieroglyphic inscriptions on stone. The wonderful ancient buildings have withstood the ravages of time; the Sphinx still looks down enigmatically upon the tourists. But we know of the golden age of ancient Egypt through frescoes, inscriptions, carvings and works of art. Her brilliant history has left us many records of the part played by ships and the sea in ancient civilizations.

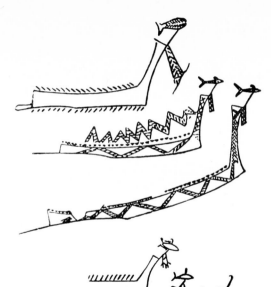

**Types of ships
as painted on vases
in the Cyclades Islands**

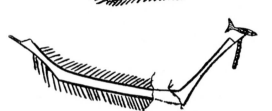

Chapter 7

THE TRADING EMPIRE

Mention of "the invaders from the great green sea" is often found in Egyptian inscriptions, and bas-reliefs show them as tall men with narrow hips and wavy hair. Their fighting equipment is very different from the Egyptians', and the gifts they bring are contained in jars and vases whose shape is quite different from Egyptian ones.

These were the Cretans. In antiquity, Crete was much more fertile and richer in natural resources than it is today. The mountains were covered with forests of pine and cypress that gave timber for building. The people cultivated the land with great care and took measures to prevent erosion. The green valleys were especially fertile; vines and olive trees abounded and gave large crops. Agriculture therefore formed the basis of the island's economy. But the export of grapes and olive oil alone could not account for its great wealth. The Cretans in fact had a high reputation for their luxury wares, and it was their manufactures and trading capabilities, far more than their agriculture, that gave them the highest standard of living in antiquity.

Many archaeologists followed Sir Arthur Evans to Crete, but however many new sites they opened up they never

Snake Goddess of Crete. Many statuettes showing her in this posture and costume have been found

unearthed, any more than Evans had, the slightest vestige of fortress walls or defense towers. Neither Knossos, the ancient center, nor Phaistos, the second largest town, was walled. What was the reason for this absence of defense works, for what has been called "the reticence of power"? The only conclusion is that the Cretans relied on another means of defense—that their powerful fleet constituted the best form of protection for their island.

Oblong-shaped Crete has a ragged coastline of about eight hundred miles, and the many bays and creeks provide good shelter for boats and fishing vessels when gales spring up. But in ancient times it was extremely difficult, because of the long coastline, to keep a constant lookout for enemy raiders. According to legend, Minos, king of the island, called upon the inventiveness of Daedalus, who had made the fabulous maze. Daedalus built

54

a giant robot of bronze, which he called Thalos, and sent it striding around the island three times a day, spitting fire at any approaching enemy and destroying him. Thalos, the first robot in history, was remembered for many generations. He was shown on Cretan coins as late as the fourth century; though, with time, he had acquired wings and been given a slim figure. (And this Thalos spat large stones instead of fire.) This legend, like so much in mythology, was symbolic: Thalos represented the powerful fleet of King Minos, whose fast ships manned with well-armed crews dealt death to any enemy who approached the island.

When Jason returned from his quest for the Golden Fleece, he was prevented from landing on Crete by the giant Thalos. But Medea, who was with her husband, knew the secret of the robot's strength—that he had a vein running from his head to the soles of his feet which contained a fluid similar to that in the bodies of the gods. Daedalus had sealed the vein with a bronze nail in one of the robot's heels. Medea, knowing all this, drew out the nail, and the life of the robot swiftly drained away.

In this myth we are presented with an allegory describing not only the might of ancient Crete and the skill of its people, but also their decline and final disaster. We can also see in it the prosperity of Minoan Crete, the power of its fleet, the wealth of its industry and trade. When the fleet was no more, industrial and commercial activities collapsed.

The Cretans differed from other Mediterranean peoples by the development of their industry, which probably resulted from their agricultural activities, particularly the making of

Seals from Crete

olive oil. On the Egyptian reliefs showing Cretans bringing gifts to the pharaoh, each "trade delegation" is headed by bearers of huge jars or pots of olive oil. The great palace at Knossos contained warehouses in which long rows of these huge jars were stored. Many have been found elsewhere on the island, and even in Greece. Evans, who was fond of making calculations, reckoned that the jars in the Knossos palace had contained fifteen thousand gallons of olive oil.

The cloth woven by the Cretans was famed all over the ancient world. The great demand for it was due not only to its quality but also to the flecked colors and beauty of its decoration. The Cretans had the secret of making purple dye, a color held in high esteem in ancient times. Purple cloth was long considered a sign of good taste and elegance, and even of great wealth.

The good ladies of Mycenae had more than one reason for being eager to possess Cretan purple cloth. The Greeks later became keen competitors for the raw materials with which purple dye was made, in order to engage in this lucrative trade themselves.

The Cretans also drew a considerable part of their wealth from the forests. Carpentry tools found during excavations provide evidence that timber and finished wood constituted one of the island's industries. But there was no marble on the island, whereas it was found in abundance on most of the Aegean islands. A few copper mines existed on Crete, however, and these were apparently exploited during the Minoan era, although they were not very rich.

Just when and how bronze first appeared in Crete is not yet known. But it is certain that all the bronze work found on the island was made locally. The bronze jewelry of Crete enjoyed a high reputation. The fact that much is found in all the countries of the Mediterranean basin is evidence of this. Bronze weapons —a specialty of the Cretans—were also exported in great numbers, not only to Greece and the islands but all over the Mediterranean and even to central Europe and beyond.

One of the most important of Cretan industries, if not taking pride of place, was pottery. Cretan jars and vases were all the rage in the ancient world, for this was a specialized craft—not surprisingly, considering that the island's potters had been working in clay for centuries. These artisans had become extremely skillful at baking clay and shaping and decorating vases. Cretan vases of the late period are distinctive by the originality of their shape and the beauty of their decorative styles. Even today they are wonderful to look at; their decorative motifs, on a background of white and yellow, purple and dark brown, are nearly always drawn from scenes in the daily life of the people—sport or games, dancing, storytelling, etc.

All these industrial activities inevitably led the Cretans to seek new markets and expand their trade; and the island's

Seals showing ships from Crete

position made it a natural middleman for the countries around the eastern Mediterranean. The Cretans were never conquerors, but essentially traders who penetrated into other countries with the most pacific of intentions, to sell manufactured goods that people greatly needed. These wise and prudent methods allowed them to extend their influence everywhere and to establish trading posts in quite distant regions. It sometimes happened, even in those ancient times, that benefits were given in exchange for trading concessions. Thucydides, writing of Minos, commented: "He even wiped out pirates, as much as he possibly could, in order to increase his trade revenues."

Thucydides, who was scrupulous in verifying the old tales still in circulation, came to a conclusion which archaeologists some two thousand four hundred years later also arrived at— that there had been a trading power in the Mediterranean that was the first maritime power ever known.

The Cretans were bound to become a seafaring race. Their future depended on the sea, which exerted a perpetual fascination . . . on the blue horizon were the outlines of other islands. . . . The young men grew up with the call of the sea in their blood; they knew the language of the wind and the waves, knew their seasonal habits and the signs of a sudden change in the weather.

Then, as now, a seaman could sail the whole length of the Mediterranean without losing his bearings, for the numerous headlands and islands serve admirably as direction posts. In the Aegean the profusion of islands almost reduces navigation to a simple ferry service. At night, the Cretans learned to guide by the stars. They became used to the solitude of the sea, to its changing

57

moods and its immensity. They were not afraid to venture farther into the unknown, to discover overseas markets and so improve their own living standards.

The Cretan ships were quite different from the Egyptians', whose lines always recalled those of the river punts out of which they had developed. Although slow and of relative seaworthiness, Egyptian ships nevertheless made long voyages. But Egypt was never a maritime power. She had little need to be. The fleet built by Tuthmosis III was used for military purposes, to carry troops, not merchandise. The pharaohs did not need ships in order to enrich themselves. But it was a very different matter with the Cretans. They could expand their economy only by trading overseas.

Gigantic jars from the palace at Knossos

There was no lack of timber on Crete in ancient times, and stout ships could be built from the pines and cypresses that covered the mountain slopes. The early Cretan ships were long and narrow, with graceful, tapering lines—similar to the tall, slim figures of their builders. They had a high forecastle, which enabled the crew to jump ashore and tie up more easily. From the prow flew the flag of the Cretan merchant fleet—the

58

outline of a fish. All Cretan ships in fact were given this distinctive marking. Thus the islanders acknowledged the basis of their wealth.... The ships had a row of oars on each side, and the bulwarks were low in order to facilitate loading and unloading. A long paddle at the stern served as a rudder; the one mast was placed well forward.

In the course of time and as the Cretans gained experience, they began to deck over their ships, and eventually the deck stretched from stem to stern. The rowers were then placed below deck. A second paddle was added at the stern, the two were linked together, and another mast was fitted; some ships were even given three masts, all quite tall, for the Cretans had realized that the wind could often speed the ship much faster than men at the oars. A fresco has even been found showing a ship without oars.

These seafarers soon grasped the essentials of navigation and the possibilities of masts and sails, and were able to make for distant shores in their search for overseas markets.

Let us imagine ourselves following one of these Cretans as he ventures ever farther across the sea . . .

Helped by a southerly breeze, he first reached the nearest island, Thira. There he saw local wares and some from Sira and other of the Cyclades. His naturally keen eye for fine merchandise was drawn to the vases from Sira . . . a high price would be asked for them, no doubt, but he had enough Cretan wares in his ship to barter for some of them.

He thus soon learned the comparative value of different articles. When he next sailed to Thira it was to sell rather than to buy. A connection was gradually established. The people of Thira appreciated Cretan products, and the seafaring hawker cornered the island market. While doing business there, he came across articles made from obsidian—vitreous lava. These were from the neighboring island of Melos, which had a monopoly of the industry. The Cretan had never been to Melos. It was believed to be inhabited by a half-savage tribe, but what risk was there in going and trying to establish a trade connection? It was tempting . . . if he managed to barter some of his Cretan products for those of Melos, and then disposed of them on the Greek mainland, to the people of Mycenae or Tiryns, he would make a considerable profit. And so his business flourished. One voyage led to another, ever more distant, and his wealth increased. One after the other, many of the Aegean islands came within his trading orbit—Delos, Naxos, Tinos, and dozens of smaller islands. Progressing from island to island, he at last

59

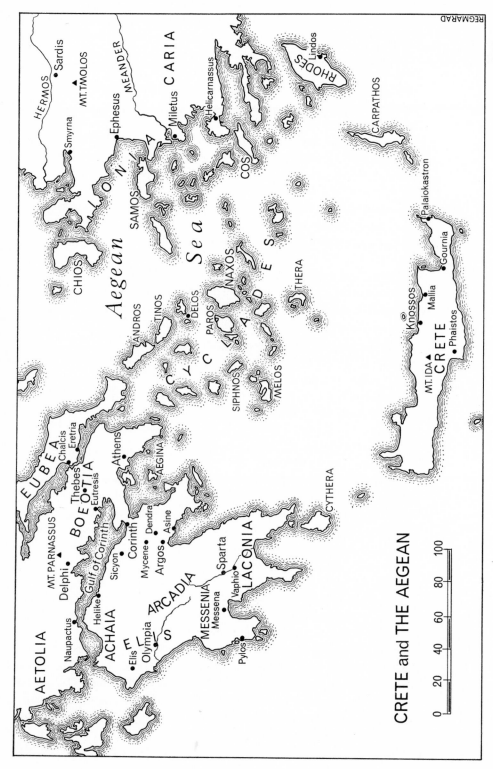

Map of Crete and the Aegean

CRETE and THE AEGEAN

reached the mainland and sold his lovely vases to the peoples of Boeotia and Arcadia.

In later years the Cretan sailed to Egypt, to countries of the Near East and even to western Mediterranean lands. He brought back from one expedition some weapons made of a new and wonderful metal—bronze. He returned with ivory statuettes too; and many kinds of jewelry and ornaments for the head, the neck, arms, fingers, and even ankles and feet. The Cretan had by then a highly developed commercial sense, an awareness of human weaknesses and foibles. He was astute enough to discover that by displaying his prettily colored wares he incited people to buy and aroused their natural desire for ornamentation, especially among women. Thus all the peoples with whom he came into contact acquired a taste for the finer things. And, repeated on a wider and larger scale, all this brought immense benefit to the Cretans as a whole.

Sooner or later it occurred to some sea-trading Cretan that he would save a lot of time and expense by stocking his wares on a centrally situated island instead of returning to Crete each time he needed more merchandise. This would enable him to give his clients better service, too, as well as reducing the risks from bad weather. Perhaps the idea came when one of the sudden and violent Mediterranean storms was tossing his ship about dangerously, and he seemed likely to lose a valuable cargo, if not his life. By establishing a center of operations on an island farther north he would more easily be able to trade on the Greek mainland and penetrate to the heart of the country.

In such a manner the Cretans reached Pylos—as Homer notes in his song to Apollo: "Many and persistent are the men of Crete. From Knossos the Minoan they set out on their affairs in a black ship, and arrived at Pylos to trade with the people there." They reached Laconia and Arcadia too; in fact they traded everywhere, and the artistry of their wares influenced the tastes of their customers. It was the Cretans who spread an idea of luxury and caused ornaments and styles to be imitated. The history of art and industry over the whole of this region began on Crete and reached its peak in Greece.

The Cretans were the first traders to reach Egypt, and the history of the two peoples intermingled for many centuries. The inhabitants of the island "in the Green Sea" are often mentioned in Egyptian records, sometimes with a touch of respect and awe.

There is evidence that Cretans visited Egypt in the time of the pharaohs Snefru and Sahura, around 2700 B.C. They were apparently fascinated by everything they saw in the gaudy river kingdom, which was then the economic and cultural center of the ancient world. The islanders were greatly interested in the possibilities, too . . . . The Egyptians had ivory statuettes, spices, ostrich feathers, gems from India, colored glass, alabaster vases —all rare and costly things—as well as gold and silver objects. What profits could be made from selling such treasures in the islands and on the Greek mainland! The people there had never seen such wonders. And the Cretans sailed for home with a precious cargo to be traded in distant lands.

It was not just trade that the Cretans acquired from Egypt. Over the years they gained knowledge and ideas from the frescoes and sculpture, the vases and jewelry in the temples and palaces, and they learned something of Egyptian techniques. From importing Egyptian luxury products they progressed to a native manufacture of them, but with an originality of style and decoration. In time, their creative ability enabled them to surpass the Egyptians and to offer them Cretan work more beautiful than their own. There was thus an interflow of ideas, a long period of exchanges between Crete and Egypt.

An experienced archaeologist like Evans, sensitive to the appearance of new shapes and decorative styles, was greatly helped in his delimitation of Cretan history by the discoveries of Egyptian origin.

It is now an accepted convention to follow Evans in his subdivision of Cretan history into four periods:

The Neolithic or New Stone Age, lasting from about 9000 to 3000 B.C. No knowledge of Egypt then existed. The many stone tools found on the island indicate that there were relations with the nearest of the Cyclades.

The Early Minoan Period, lasting until about 1800 B.C. This was the Bronze Age period of Crete, during which the industries of the island were gradually developed, transforming the life of the people. Objects found that date from this period are of Egyptian origin and enabled Evans to make a sharp delimitation of the period.

The Middle Minoan Period, lasting from 1800 to 1600 B.C., was the time when Cretan power and civilization came to a peak. It was also the period of Egypt's rapid decline, when the Hyksos were ruling the country. Disaster came to Crete, too. A severe earthquake, about 1700 B.C., caused extensive damage, the town of Knossos being completely destroyed. However, the great energy of the Cretans enabled them to overcome these misfortunes. Knossos was rebuilt, and other reconstruction was

Glazed pottery vase from Phaistos

prompt and complete, indicating both social and political stability as well as great wealth. Indeed, the economic and artistic activities of the Cretans shortly afterward reached their highest level.

The Late Minoan Period, which ended about 1450 B.C. in an overwhelming disaster. Until then, this was the "golden age" of Crete. The islanders had almost a monopoly of trade over a wide area, and their living standards were higher than any other peoples, in the ancient world. But the Cretans made no recovery, this time, from what is still an unexplained, sudden catastrophe. The great period in Cretan history came to a close.

Much evidence from Egyptian sources exists about the commercial and friendly relations between the Egyptians and the "Keftiu" during the latter's golden age.

The Cretans fully realized that to do good business with other races it was necessary to be on good terms with them. Cretans are shown on Egyptian frescoes as vassals paying tribute to their masters. But this was just Egyptian vanity—the pharaoh ruled the world, so there could not be any tribe or people exonerated from paying tribute to him. The Egyptian painters, sculptors and scribes flattered their master and paid tribute with their art. Throughout the long history of Cretan relations with Egypt, which spread over fifteen centuries, the islanders in fact received favorable treatment compared with other peoples.

Tuthmosis III established sound relations with the Cretans. The following inscription has been discovered on the tomb of the pharaoh's military chief of staff Rekhmare: "We received gifts from the kings of Keftiu and the islands, which are out in the middle of the sea." There is also mention of a present sent by Rekhmare, a gold vase, "to gladden the heart of the king."

The Cretans were therefore far from being vassals of the Egyptians. To conquer the island the pharaohs would have had to build a strong fleet and fight a naval battle. But Egypt had no fleet until the reign of Tuthmosis III, and then it was used to transport troops to Syria. Moreover, Tuthmosis is known to have made use of Keftiu ships to bring timber from Lebanon for the building of his fleet. The Cretans grew wealthy not only from importing and exporting but also from engaging in the sea-carrying trade. They became specialists, and proof of this is found in the gifts received from various pharaohs.

PLATE 4

**Egyptian warship of the reign of Ramses III,
twelfth century B.C.**

Model designed by M. Milch and built by M. I. Krupnik, of
Haifa Maritime Museum, from low relief at Medinet-Abou,
representing the triumph of Ramses III over the Peoples of the
Sea, who included the Philistines, in a naval battle. The Peoples
of the Sea assembled and fitted out their fleets in the Aegean
islands for their attempted conquest of Egypt by way of the
Nile Delta.

The hull of this vessel is long and pointed, with high bulwarks
intended to protect the galley slaves who rowed it in action.
This type of warship, like all other Egyptian ships, is still without
a keel, which is replaced by the same device as in previous
examples. It has a square sail and nine oars on each side. The
most interesting detail is the figurehead: the head of a lion
holding a human head in its jaws, instead of the more familiar
lotus flower.

PLATE 4

Egyptian warship of the Reign of Ramses III
twelfth century B.C

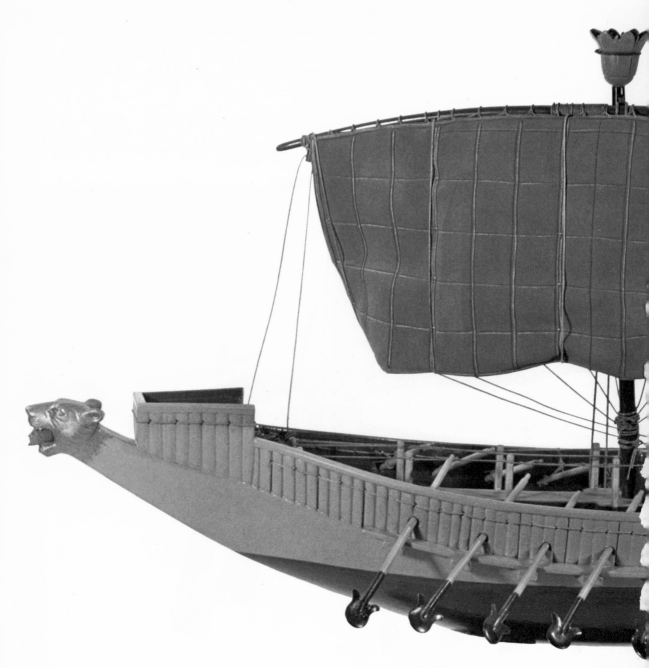

Seal from Crete with combined horse and ship designs

Chapter 8

TRADE ROUTES AND SEA MONSTERS

The Cretans' success in establishing a wide network of trading posts and bases was due to the peaceful and diplomatic means they employed. An archaeologist who was an underwater specialist made the amazing discovery, early in the present century, of the remains of a harbor dating back to the eighteenth century B.C. on the island of Pharos, just off Alexandria. It covered sixty acres and was protected by a jetty over a mile long and thirty to sixty yards wide. The harbor had been divided by a quay fifteen yards wide, and there had been a warehouse almost half a mile in length.

The ancient Egyptians certainly had no use for such a large harbor and installations, although the work was no doubt carried out by Egyptian labor. But work and human lives were cheap in the Nile valley. The Cretans were the only people capable of planning such a harbor and then putting it to good use. The Egyptians must nevertheless have drawn considerable revenues from the goods passing through it, for the Cretans were prepared to pay well in order to increase their markets.

The whole "international" trading and carrying was eventually in the hands of the Cretans. The "gold of the northern seas"— amber—was conveyed overland from Jutland and the Baltic by a long and tortuous route to the head of the Adriatic, to the market center of Aquileia (present-day Venice). From there it was carried south and east by Cretan traders, who were well aware of the fondness of princes and their ladies for the yellow substance. Aquileia was a meeting place for merchants of many different peoples. There the Cretans came into contact with Teutons and Scandinavians, tall men with fair hair and blue

65

Cretan seal

eyes; with merchants from Styria (Austria), dark-haired men who had a wonderful, rare substance called salt among their wares. There were broad-shouldered Etruscans and slim, long-haired Slavs. All brought their particular specialties to sell or to exchange for others. The Cretans, however, had no specialty; they dealt in everything, and this was their strength as traders. They bartered gems from Egypt for amber from the north, Cretan vases for salt, and so on. Then they loaded their ships with these riches from the north and sailed to markets in the south and east. Egypt was an important junction on the trade routes. The Cretans exported their manufactured products to Egypt, and even their Keftiu herbs, which were much in demand for pharmaceutical preparations.

Cretan ships eventually made their way to Cyprus—then known as Alassia—and established trading posts. The copper mines of Cyprus were well known. The Cretans not only bought copper, they learned how to make bronze from it and then sold the finished product. They also established bases on Carpathos, Rhodes, and Cos, and from these islands were able to trade with the peoples of Asia Minor.

The Cretans enjoyed friendly relations with Troy—the famous war did not break out until the Greeks had supplanted the Cretans. In fact the causes of the Trojan war sprang from trade rivalry far more than from the loves of Helen.

From Cyprus the Cretans had but a short sea passage to Byblos (ex-Gebal) where they traded papyrus from Egypt. (The Bible gets its name from Byblos, for it was first written on papyrus imported through that port.) The many and varied trading activities of the Cretans have left their traces all over the eastern Mediterranean. They were the first to introduce

66

the Arab horse into Europe, via Crete. At a later date they were responsible for the spread of an Eastern invention, the wheeled cart. They introduced it to their island, and this led to the making of a system of roads linking the towns, many traces of which still exist. But the greatest achievement of the Cretans was in the production of bronze articles, though it was probably not they who invented the metal, since it was more likely to have happened in a country where copper and tin were found. But the best bronzes and the spread of bronze products were undoubtedly due to the Cretans. Bronze was of great importance to the ancients and a major factor in the advance of civilization. The Cretans would not have failed to draw immense advantage and profit from it.

Tin was found chiefly in Spain, usually in the neighborhood of copper and silver mines. Silver objects of Spanish origin dating from 2500 B.C. have been found in Crete, though this does not necessarily mean that Cretans reached Spain at such an early date. The silver may have been obtained at some market center, possibly Aquileia. In any case it is clear that Cretans paid visits to Spain early in the second millennium, and may even have passed beyond the Straits of Gibraltar to the tin and silver emporium of Tartessus, which lay at or near the mouth of the Guadalquivir. They reached the western Mediterranean through the Straits of Messina. Traces of their presence in Sicily have been discovered all over that large island. Among the many legends connected with Sicily is one indicating that the island was colonized by Cretans. King Minos is said to have met his death in Sicily while in pursuit of Daedalus. Daedalus had taught the Sicilians how to make bronze, and they soon developed the industry with the object of becoming independent of Crete. King Minos saw this as a danger to Cretan economy and attempted to restrain the Sicilians ... but they killed him.

Cretan legends were handed down from one generation to the next. The Greek historian Diodorus began his book on Sicily with the story of the murder of Minos by the daughters of King Cocalus. The Cretans retaliated by invading Sicily and laying siege to the capital, Camicos. The siege lasted five years, but was unsuccessful. Herodotus took the tale further: the besiegers withdrew, for there was sickness and hunger in their ranks, and sailed away from the island. A violent storm sprang up and most of the ships were sunk. The survivors reached the coast of southern Italy and founded colonies there. One of the towns was called Minoa, in remembrance of King Minos. (This was a name adopted in many parts of the Mediterranean, an indication that Cretans had established good relations with the inhabitants of the area.)

Diodorus, however, has the survivors of the Cretan force remaining on Sicily to found colonies. He wrote that the Cretan colonies in southern Italy were founded by the Greek hero Theseus, who fled from Knossos with a group of young men and girls after killing the Minotaur.

In any case, the decoration on pottery which has been unearthed, and ancient customs mentioned by early travelers, tend to support the theory that these legends had their basis in historical fact.

Discoveries on Sardinia, too, indicate Cretan penetration at a period when the production of bronze was in its infancy. Sardinia seems to have enjoyed great prosperity and a high standard of living in those remote times. There is even a legend that the Sardinians attempted to invade Crete, but were terrified by the giant Thalos (whose mockery of them is said to be the origin of "sardonic laughter").

To deter other seafarers from competing in their markets, especially from following in their wake to distant Tartessus, where an abundance of precious tin could be obtained, the Cretans had a simple yet effective means: the spreading of stories which put fear and dread into the minds of others. The Cretans knew the route to the Straits of Gibraltar and beyond, but woe to any seafarers who took the same route. They would be set upon by sea monsters and destroyed, ships and all! This means of putting fear into others was a favorite ruse in antiquity. A typical example is the story of Scylla and Charybdis, monsters occupying rocks on either side of the Straits of Messina. Scylla had six heads and a dozen arms, and lay in wait in that dreaded spot, ready to devour sailors and crush their ships. But that was not the only danger. On the opposite side was Charybdis, who swallowed down the waters and then threw them up again.

Great courage was needed to sail through those dreadful narrows. Odysseus, it will be remembered, avoided having his ship gulped down by Charybdis, but "Scylla meanwhile caught from out my ship six of my company . . . and devoured them . . ." while Odysseus was unable to prevent it.

There were many other frightening tales, all designed to strike terror into the minds of listeners. The Cretans naturally had no fear of Scylla or Charybdis, or of any of the other monsters described in imaginary tales. The Cretans continued

Odysseus bound to the mast by his own orders, to save him from the temptation of the Sirens

to sail through the Straits of Messina and to journey farther west in search of cargoes of tin.

However, there came a time when the tin mines of southern Spain were becoming worked out. Bronze objects were in great demand everywhere, and so an ever-increasing supply of tin was needed. Tin, in those times, had a place in world economics similar to that of oil at the present day. New supplies of tin were discovered in northwest France and in Cornwall. It is difficult to believe that Cretan ships sailed to these shores, yet evidence has been found in many places attesting to visits by Cretans. The Greek word "kasiteros," meaning tin, originates from a Celtic term for "far distant islands." But more to the point is the fact that Cretan jewelry and silver money weights have been discovered in the neighborhood of Plymouth.

This discovery also indicates that the Cretans used a form of money. They had probably realized that their many trading operations in different lands had made necessary some system of a unit weight or monetary measure—that bartering no longer sufficed. A unit of value, recognized as such by all peoples, was the solution to a complicated bartering process. Aristotle put the matter succinctly: "There should be a common value for all things used as articles of exchange. Silver would do very well. Silver has a weight and equal value. It determines the worth of one thing in relation to another, the number of pairs of sandals that represent the value of a house. It determines the worth of a mason's work in relation to that of a sandal maker, the number of pairs of sandals to be given for a house." The repetitions are not Aristotle's fault. He expressed his ideas to his pupils, and it was they who wrote them down.

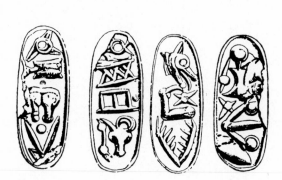

Brooches and seals from Crete

If the Cretans did not invent money, they were very likely the people who first spread the idea of using an international monetary measure. Plates of raw copper shaped like a bull's head have been discovered in various places, and these almost certainly served the Cretans as money. But what was the backing for their currency? The palace at Knossos certainly did not contain a hoard of gold like that held at the Bank of England or at Fort Knox. There can be only one answer to explain why Cretan money was accepted by the Cornish tin miner, the Jutland amber merchant, the Memphis jeweler and the Aegean potter—it was the confidence they all had in the power and wealth of Crete. The value of its money was known to be stable; traders the world over used Cretan money as a common currency.

One example of how deeply the belief in the legendary power and stability of the Cretans was ingrained in other peoples is provided by the following fact: when the Philistines invaded Egypt more than two centuries after the disappearance of Crete

70

as a merchant power, the coffers of the invaders held . . . Cretan money. Such is the wonderful effect of legends.

So King Minos and his people established the first "thalassocracy," or dominion of the seas, and the first merchant empire in world history. Wherever raw materials were to be had, wherever possibilities for the middleman existed, there the Cretans were to be found. These seafarers and traders were always prepared to buy, transport, sell or exchange goods. Their power derived from their boldness and initiative, their inventive and organizing abilities, trading sense and artistic tastes. They created a new civilization, more refined and progressive. Everywhere they went, their influence led primitive and semibarbarous peoples to adopt a more cultivated existence. The Cretans were marveled at—but envied too. The mainland peoples were astounded at the immense accumulated wealth of the island kingdom. The name of Knossos, the Lady of the Seas,

"Milk stones" from Crete

had such a strong hold over the imagination of the Mediterranean people that even fourteen centuries after the final destruction Virgil had his hero Aeneas return to Crete, to the cradle of the tribe. . . . Homer, too, in his description of Odysseus meeting lovely Nausicaa and being favorably received at the king's palace, probably had in mind the tales of the delightful, cultivated life at Knossos, tales which had lost none of their splendor in being handed down through many generations.

The ancients had a belief that Crete was the lost continent of Atlantis, and they continued to believe so for a long time, although Plato clearly indicated that Atlantis was beyond the Pillars of Hercules. For centuries, people were fascinated by the wonderful tales of hidden treasures on the island, of its fabulous fleet and great wealth. People have always felt drawn toward symbols of riches. It is not surprising that Crete was associated with the Utopia of Greek sea power.

The power of the Cretans was due to the sea, and so was the calamity that came upon them. If they had stayed on their island, keeping themselves to themselves, they would have aroused no one's envy. If their ships had been used only for

71

guarding the approaches to the island, no invader could have landed to plunder the towns.

How fascinating is the history of ancient Crete! It is the original elements in the civilization that account for the special appeal and interest: there is the evidence of writing at a very early date, the Linear A and B scripts, of which only the latter has been read, and even that imperfectly; and there is the lack of walled defenses, and the artistry and vigor of the people. This remarkably advanced and exciting civilization still remains something of an enigma. . . .

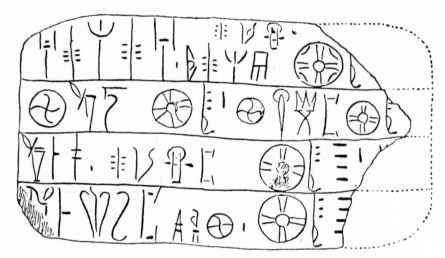

A tablet from Knossos, in the so-called Linear B script, being a catalog of stores or merchandise

Mount Ida, the island's 8,000-foot peak, is still a landmark to seafarers—other seafarers, in very different ships. When the sun glints on her snow-crowned summit she seems to be flashing defiance to all men—in your vanity you thought to discover my hidden secrets, but they are buried deep in my grottoes, under the now bare slopes and the sea at my feet. Will you ever succeed in uncovering all the secrets concealed within me?

The overwhelming disaster that came to Crete left wide expanses of sea empty of ships. But before long another race of seafarers had taken the place of the Cretans, inheriting their traditions of seamanship and knowledge of the trade routes, and equaling them in self-sacrifice and daring. These newcomers were the Phoenicians.

The oldest known model of a ship, from Eridu

Chapter 9

THE GATES TO

THE MEDITERRANEAN

No sooner has one sea power been submerged in the backwater of history than another appears on the horizon. For the sea is the natural link between peoples; since time immemorial they have used the seaways to exchange their products for other essentials. The sea can never remain empty of ships.

The Cretan flag bearing its symbolic fish was no longer seen on the deep blue sea. The new overlords of the island, people from Mycenaean Greece, sailed only in waters known to them, plying to the Aegean islands and their native land. They may have touched in along the coast of Asia Minor, but that was as far as they felt it necessary to venture outside home waters.

For a time, maritime enterprise lay dormant. But a day came when a squat, wide-beamed ship laden with merchandise from many parts could have been seen sailing slowly along some western Mediterranean shore. She was not alone; the accompanying ship was narrow and sleek, built for speed, and carried armed men. The cargo ship had an escort. These were the Phoenicians, a Semitic people.

Professor Toynbee, who is not exactly favorably inclined

73

toward the Semites, acknowledges nevertheless that mankind is indebted to them for three things: they developed writing, they discovered the Atlantic (thus greatly widening man's horizons), and they enriched spiritual life by spreading the doctrine of monotheism.

It is only in quite recent times that archaeology has thrown some light on the history of the Phoenicians, who were previously regarded as the mystery people of antiquity. Even so, the knowledge we have has been drawn largely from non-Phoenician sources, which are therefore open to discussion. Egyptian inscriptions—always disdainful of everyone not Egyptian—mention the Phoenicians in an airy and cursory manner. The Bible treats the Phoenicians as idolaters, and this determined the attitude of the prophets toward them (or the Canaanites, the name the Hebrews gave them). Greek sources are almost entirely one-sided. The Greeks were for many centuries trade rivals of the Phoenicians, so it is not surprising that the picture they drew of the latter should be unflattering to them. Although the Greeks acknowledged among themselves that their rivals were fine navigators and explorers and worthy traders, they had no hesitation in describing the Phoenicians as knaves and sea scavengers.

Homer refers to the Phoenicians as fine seamen but hypocrites, whose ships were loaded with many wondrous things. These hypocrites and sea scavengers are now recognized as having been the greatest seafarers in antiquity, whose ships sailed into every sea and whose goods were found in every port. Yet records of them are surprisingly scanty. These traders who dealt

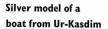

Silver model of a boat from Ur-Kasdim

74

in everything were in fact exporters of cultural and spiritual values. They did not invent the alphabet or writing, but improved on hieroglyphics and imported the art of writing to peoples with whom they traded. Herodotus admitted that they were the first to introduce the alphabet into Greece.

There can be no doubt that the contribution of the Phoenicians to the advance of civilization was considerable. Yet they left singularly few records of themselves and their virtues. They were, and remained, essentially middlemen. Even in intellectual matters they were not creative but continued in their role of intermediaries. It was chiefly their realism that differentiated them from other peoples of antiquity. They drew up rules of trade and established conventions. Their reasons for introducing writing to others were entirely practical: it enabled merchants and traders everywhere to keep proper accounts and to communicate the state of their stocks. The Phoenicians were no doubt guided by motives of material gain, but that does not lessen mankind's debt to them. Civilization made great advances at this period through the enterprise of traders.

The Phoenicians were regarded, not surprisingly, as people without a country, as seafarers who considered that any place where life was good and pleasant was the place to stay. Such in fact was their attitude. However, this limited view of the Phoenicians is of no great help in determining the truth about them. There is evidence that on more than one occasion they proved themselves devoted to their city-kingdoms, and were prepared to make sacrifices for their homeland. Recorded history is not at all objective about the Phoenicians; the ancients were no more generous-minded toward their enemies and rivals than the moderns.

Some specialists have advanced the theory that the Phoenicians were descendants of Cretans who established colonies in the Near East subsequent to the forming of trade relations. This theory is based on the fact that the Cretan traditions of seamanship and aptitude for trading passed to the Phoenicians. But this convenient explanation is hardly good enough. It is known that before the final disaster to Knossos the scribes kept the palace records in the Greek language. So that if the Phoenicians originated from Crete, some traces of the island's culture, religion or legends ought to have come to light in what was ancient Phoenicia. Such is not the case.

Herodotus would have us believe that the Phoenicians originated from lands along the Persian Gulf. In the course of their wanderings they reached the Mediterranean and founded

Tyre, many generations before the Trojan War. Herodotus visited Tyre about 450 B.C., and met priests who were serving in the temple of the god Melkart. It was from them that he heard that the temple and the town had first been built twenty-three centuries before his visit. These tales, like all those of the ancients, were wrapped up in legends and myths. One was about the Nefilims, the demigods who reigned on earth after the Creation. Among their number was the great hunter Usoos—as he is called in Greek myths—who was the father of all seafarers. He put to sea on a tree trunk and was carried to a small island off the coast of Syria, or Phoenicia. The great hunter—whose name symbolized strength and daring—set up two pillars on the island, one being dedicated to fire and the other to the wind. (They were probably pillars of sacrifice to the gods personifying the forces of nature.) Then Usoos founded the religious cult of the Phoenicians by offering sacrifices on the altar he built in the city of Tyre.

Another of the legends has it that Tyre was built on a site that had once been an island. A giant olive tree, sacred to the goddess Astarte, grew on the island. It was guarded by a serpent and a powerful eagle. Some hero had to kill the eagle and sacrifice it to the gods, and then the island would cease drifting about the sea. Usoos performed the brave deed, and the island became joined to the mainland. Tyre was then built upon it, and the gods watched over the peace and happiness of the city. A temple was set up to the god Melkart and a sanctuary for the goddess Astarte.

These legends, like those of many other ancient peoples, undoubtedly relate to the mysteries of the Creation.

There seems little doubt from present evidence that the Phoenicians came originally from the region between the Tigris and the Euphrates, as did the Semitic peoples in general. A migration from this region began early in the third millennium and by the twenty-third century B.C. had attained vast proportions. Whole tribes were making their way south and west toward Egypt, some from beyond the Euphrates, from Elam and Persia. A conqueror from the northern half of Babylonia, Sargon the Akkadian, swept south and established his rule over Sumer. He then extended his conquests westward, and is said to have reached the Mediterranean and sent sea expeditions from Phoenicia to raid Cyprus and Crete. It has even been maintained by some imaginative modern writers, on the strength of supposed Babylonian place names in Spain, that this country was colonized from Mesopotamia. But the improbability is

76

enormous; the evidence of Babylonian derivations of Spanish names is extremely slender. And it is most unlikely that Sargon ever raided Crete. On the other hand, there is no doubt of the great migration of Semitic tribes in Sargon's time. Some

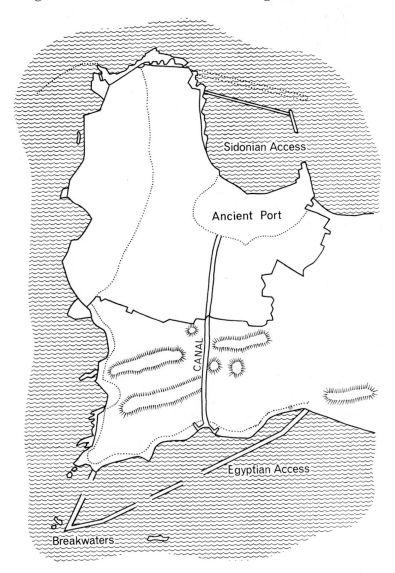

Sketch map of Tyre and its harbor, showing breakwaters constructed in the sea by the Tyreans

penetrated into Asia Minor and established a number of kingdoms, from one of which came the Hyksos who succeeded in making themselves masters of Egypt and ruled over that country for one hundred and fifty years.

Canaan, or Phoenicia, became a crossroads where various powerful tribes seeking to expand met and clashed. Some

77

Phoenician seal

occupied the coastal areas, which were easy of access to wandering tribes as roads existed between inhabited places. The general movement of peoples at this period was due either to a desire for conquest or to an increasing population. The latter meant—as it still does for many countries—that there would be famine and death in the land. The areas to the west, bordering the Mediterranean, however, were largely available to new populations. Certainly they were much less inhabited than the regions around the Persian Gulf and between the Tigris and the Euphrates.

Modern scholars are divided over the early history of the Phoenicians and the part they played in opening up the Mediterranean. In any case, they had close contact with the Egyptians from very early times. The latter, whose vanity was not the least of their defects, were scornful of the Phoenicians, whose living conditions seemed very poor—their roads were bad, their drinking water unhealthy, and the men "always had their feet on the move," to quote an Egyptian scribe. There can be no doubt that the Egyptians, who were used to permanent housing in splendid surroundings, felt nothing but disdain for the wandering proclivities and primitive conditions of the Phoenicians. The Semites, however, did not take long to adapt the benefits of Egyptian civilization to their own needs, and in some matters excelled their masters. By about 1800 B.C. their leaders were being addressed as "nobles" and "princes" by pharaohs of the twelfth dynasty, who also sent presents as a sign of friendly relations, in particular to the princes of Gebal. The Phoenician ports of Gebal and Sidon appear to have been early Egyptian colonies. The influence of Egyptian religion can be easily detected in the Phoenician cult. The legend of the body of Osiris reaching the shores of Gebal and being gathered up by a miraculous tree was well known, and the fact of a temple to Isis being set up on the spot indicates how close were relations between Egypt and Phoenicia.

Among the many surviving stories, legends, and descriptions contained in the literature of ancient Egypt is an account of the adventures of a certain Sinuhet, a noble who was prominent at the court of Amenemhat I, founder of the twelfth dynasty. Sinuhet fled from Egypt soon after the death of this pharaoh, having plotted against his successor, Senusert I. A Canaanite tribe in Syria gave hospitality to Sinuhet, who stayed among them and eventually became a person of importance. When full of years he had a great yearning to see his own country again. Senusert forgave him and allowed him to return to Egypt, where he was received at court with full honor. He told the story of his life among the Canaanites, giving a full description of their everyday activities, their customs and religious ceremonies, details of their social and political organization and military

common type of Phoenician ship, believed to be modeled on the Cretan prototype. The figurehead may have something to do with the symbolism of the seal on page 65

79

techniques. He also gave an account of the weapons and tools they used, of their agricultural methods and their system of irrigation. In short, his story is firsthand historical evidence of a rare kind, since it provides information on all aspects of the life of a wandering Semite tribe in Syria hundreds of centuries before the Christian era.

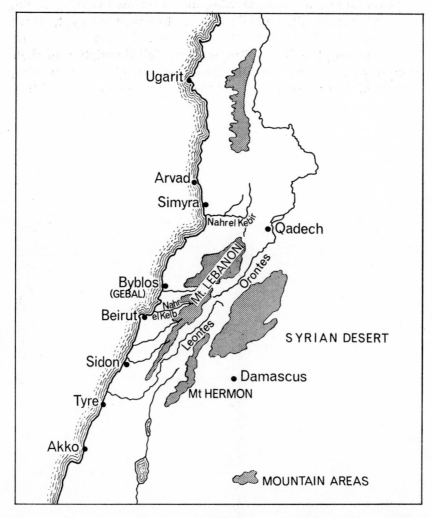

Sketch map of Phoenicia

An additional matter of interest in this account is the change of attitude toward the Phoenicians which can be discerned. This was probably due to Egypt's increasing need of good timber, to make coffins as well as to build ships. Their burial customs called for strongly made coffins that would resist the encroachment of time, and for cedar oil, myrrh, and various unguents necessary for embalming corpses. All these, particularly

80

PLATE 5

Philistine warship of the twelfth century B.C.

This is a prototype reconstructed from a mural engraving at Medinet-Abou which showed a sea fight between the Egyptian fleet and that of the Peoples of the Sea. The Philistines in their expansive phase spread out in successive waves in search of suitable points for colonization, including the southeastern corner of the Mediterranean. They installed themselves in southern Syria and the land of Canaan, and from there made efforts to invade Egypt by landings in the Nile Delta. Ramses III made war on them and expelled them from his domains. The engraving on which this model is based was made to commemorate the victory of the Egyptians over the Philistines. It has a single square sail fixed to a mainmast which is of singletree type. There is an identical figurehead, representing a goose, at prow and stern. The hull is bluff-built at both ends, and the only difference between prow and stern is in the ram which appears forward. Its presence implies a keel of conventional type. Steering is by a pair of steering oars, not fixed to each other but pivoted on either quarter of the poop. There is a crow's nest for a lookout at the top of the mast.

PLATE 5

Philistine warship of the twelfth century B.C.

Lebanon cedar, the Phoenicians had. So it was better to put aside national pride and treat those uncouth, contemptible tribes as though they were the equals of Egyptians.

There was also the fact that the Phoenicians' living conditions greatly improved when they ceased their wanderings and settled down. Later, they began to learn the art of shipbuilding from the Egyptians. The latter liked their comforts and had a distinct inclination toward laziness. So why should they fetch timber from Phoenicia and build ships when they could have ships built for them at Gebal? At first, the Phoenicians constructed their ships on the Egyptian model, but their practical sense led them to eliminate the defects and to make such advances in techniques that the "ship from Gebal" acquired a high reputation among the Egyptians.

The Phoenicians began to give their ships broad and shallow hulls which would ride comfortably on the swell and were better suited for the carrying trade. They were more seaworthy too. As experience of shipbuilding increased, Phoenician, like Cretan, vessels were decked over and had room below for a double line of rowers (usually slaves). Two large paddles fitted either side of the stern were used for steering; in ships where they were joined at the top, a kind of canopy was placed above them. A broad sail of square rig was slung from the mast that was stepped amidships and went down to the keel, while a shorter mast forward had a small sail that was used chiefly when changing course. In time, more importance was given to the sails than to oar propulsion, and both prow and stern were built higher, for this was found to facilitate mooring and making fast. As was the custom in antiquity, a banner showing an animal or some monster was flown at the prow. The Phoenicians improved the lines of their speedy ships, too, building them sleek and narrow and with a sharp, pointed prow. They were equipped with a gangway that could be let down and secured to the shore. (The Greeks and Romans, at a much later date, improved on this invention.) These were the ships known and admired in antiquity and referred to in the Old Testament as "Tarshish ships"—vessels that plied to Tartessus. They were about one hundred feet in length, and with a good wind in their sails could soon reach the other end of the Mediterranean. When the wind dropped, the rowers supplied the motive power.

The Phoenicians, unlike the Egyptians, never built any yachts or pleasure boats. They were essentially a practical people, and their ships were built only for purposes of trade.

Phoenicia was a long coastal strip extending from Asia Minor to Palestine. The various tribes had each settled around a river mouth and were separated from one another by hills and mountain slopes, so that each formed a distinct, small "kingdom" —little more than a coastal town and a few fields. It was in the valleys of the great rivers, the Nile, Tigris, and Euphrates, that different peoples had become fused into a strong political unity, a kind of nation. But the geographical factor that had determined this process did not exist in Phoenicia. The little kingdoms strung along the coast, but separated by natural barriers, often made war on each other; they did not even unite against a common enemy, as did the Greek city-states. In this respect the Phoenicians showed a lack of political sense and caused them to be easy prey for aggressive powers. On the other hand, they succeeded in maintaining a certain autonomy by adjusting themselves to the ruling power, proving pliant and adaptable. The Egyptians, however, were never harsh and pitiless masters. Several Phoenician towns realized that it was in their own interests to place themselves under the protection of Egypt, a world power and the richest market for international trade at that time. The Egyptians never tried to force their religious beliefs and practices upon the Phoenicians, or to interfere with their internal affairs. Even when Egyptian military power was at its height, the pharaohs did no more than protect the Phoenician towns against foreign aggression. And in exchange the Phoenicians supplied Egypt with timber, ships, myrrh and unguents—for cash.

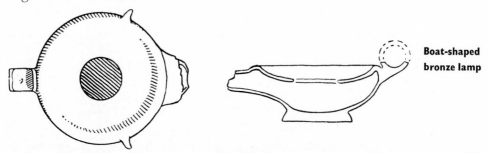

Boat-shaped
bronze lamp

The Phoenician towns developed their trade and grew prosperous; their common interests with Egypt strengthened over the centuries. While Egypt remained a dominant power, conditions in Phoenicia continued to be safe and stable, and the security of the towns—Gebal, Tyre, Sidon, Arvad, Zemer, and Acco—was assured. The most ancient of them and for long the most important was Gebal, the port from which the majority of the exports to Egypt were shipped.

The appearance of the Hittites on the scene put an end to

the era of peace and stability for Gebal. The Hittites had built up a military and political empire in the north, beyond the Taurus mountains, and were spreading their domination southward, threatening the nearest Phoenician towns, although they (the Hittites) were supposed to be under Egyptian authority.

Many years ago, at Tel el Amarna in Upper Egypt, a peasant digging his plot of ground turned up some clay tablets impressed with marks and signs. When examined by experts they were found to be ancient tablets covered with cuneiform script, a system of writing which had originated in Akkad, the northern half of Babylonia. It was the diplomatic language between the eighteenth and the fourteenth centuries B.C.; and the tablets unearthed by the peasant were part of the archives of Akhnaton I, the pharaoh who ruled in Egypt from 1375 to 1358 B.C. Akhnaton, who had changed his name from Amonophis, was an odd character. He succeeded for a time in making profound changes in Egyptian religion, displacing the powerful god of Thebes, Amon, by a deity of his own choosing, Aton the sun disk. This intellectual and dreamy pharaoh had the sensitivity of a poet, and he wrote some fine songs of praise to his particular god:

> How great are thy works
> Hidden from our eyes.
> Thou art one God, there is none other but Thee,
> Of Thine own will Thou hast created the earth,
> When Thou wast alone.

and

> Thou art the sun of the day, terror of far-off lands,
> Thou hast created life.
> Thou hast created light in the heavens.
> We bow before it.
> Waves beat against mountains in the midst of the sea,
> Fields compass their cities round about,
> How wonderful are Thy ways,
> O King eternal.

Akhnaton not only transformed the old religion, he founded a new capital, Akhetaton (the Horizon of Aton), which was built to his taste and inspiration. There he gave free play to his mysticism, dreaming of a better world, a happier life in which he would be "the king living a life of truth." Far from the tumult

83

of Thebes and the intrigues of the traditional priesthood, he there devoted himself to the pure joys of mystic contemplation and a quiet family life with his beautiful wife, Nefertiti.

Within a few years of Akhnaton's death the new capital was destroyed and deserted; but the exquisite beauty of his young wife has survived—a painted limestone bust of her is in the Berlin State Museums. Life with her visionary husband could not have been easy, though, and a bust of a later period has her looking sad and weary. In fact she died under mysterious circumstances during her husband's reign, and several Egyptologists have advanced the theory that the pharaoh had a hand in her death, in order to marry Tii, his own mother. But the history of this period is much in dispute. . . . Some imaginative writers have maintained that the story of Oedipus was taken from the life of Akhnaton. His revolt against his father, Amenophis III, his marriage with his mother, the mystery of his wife's death (no record and no tomb!), and his deliberate withdrawal from public life—all that has much in common with the tragedy of Oedipus, and could have become known to the Greeks . . . .

The years of Akhnaton's reign were the time when the Hittites were advancing south into Phoenicia, and were seriously threatening the Egyptian hold over the region. If an energetic and political realist had been on the throne, the breakup of the Egyptian empire might well have been delayed for several generations. But its pharaoh was then this dreamy idealist with a complex, this contemplative poet who cared nothing for affairs of state.

The Hittites, under their dynamic military leader Azirou, captured the northern Phoenician towns of Ugarit, Tunip, and Zemer, and marched on Gebal and Sidon. The King of Gebal, Rib-Adi, who was still loyal to Egypt, sent messengers to Akhnaton informing him of the dangerous situation and asking for military aid. Similar messages were sent to the pharaoh by Zimrida, King of Sidon, and Abi-Milki, King of Tyre, whose requests were amazingly modest—a score of soldiers and a few war chariots. Perhaps they innocently imagined that a handful of Egyptian soldiers was enough to frighten off the invaders.

Azirou, too, was sending messages to the pharaoh, and at the same time he was astute enough to try to gain friends at court by heaping presents on one of Akhnaton's chief counselors. One of Azirou's messages to the pharaoh explained that his only reason for occupying Tunip was to defend the town against an invasion by . . . Hittites. The trusting and gullible Akhnaton replied by asking Azirou to go to the aid of Zemer, too. But

Azirou claimed that as the Hittites were advancing south he
had first to defend the regions under Egyptian control that
were being directly threatened, and so he could neither go to
the help of Zemer nor appear in person before the pharaoh.
Such hypocrisy and cunning show that Azirou must have had not
only great psychological insight but also been well informed
about conditions in the Egyptian empire and the situation at
the pharaoh's court.

The King of Gebal sent over forty messages to Akhnaton
imploring help, and his demands became less modest as
enemy pressure increased. When the Hittites began a sea
blockade of Gebal he sent a despairing appeal to the pharaoh:
"Place your men in all these towns ... and stop their ships being
used against me!" The King of Gebal was probably referring to
Sidon and Arvad, which had both been captured and then
formed an alliance with the Hittites. The ships blockading Gebal
apparently came from those two ports.

Sacrificial boat

The last appeals of Rib-Adi had a pathetic tone: "The enemy
has sent his ships there. . . . It is impossible to send wheat to
Zemer, impossible to get to Zemer at all. . . ." And the King went
on to describe the dramatic siege of Zemer by land and sea. This
town soon fell to the Hittites, and then Gebal was forced to
capitulate after its ships had been seized by the enemy. Sea
communications with Egypt were cut, and Rib-Adi's worst fears
were realized.

The capture of Zemer had been largely brought about by the
attack from the sea, a new form of warfare which had taken
the town by surprise; it had no means of defense in that quarter.
The warship was beginning to take an important place in military
operations . . . .

The Phoenician towns had counted on Egyptian aid and
protection, but the reigning pharaoh was interested in other
matters. The decline of the Egyptian empire had set in, and

85

**Carved sarcophagus
from Amatos**

the Phoenicians concluded an alliance with their aggressors. The pharaohs of the nineteenth dynasty, in particular Ramses II, made energetic attempts to retrieve the situation. Ramses the Great led a strong army to Kadesh to check the advance of the Hittites, but that bloody encounter was indecisive, leading to a treaty with the barbarians—the "pirates" over whom Ramses was supposed to have won a splendid victory. In fact its splendor existed only on the walls of Egyptian temples.

After the old pharaoh's death Egypt was gravely threatened by the Peoples of the Sea, who were repulsed only at great cost in lives and devastated towns. Among these invaders were the Philistines, who had settled in southern Palestine. From that region their armies were spreading north and south along the coast, striking dread into the hearts of their enemies, for these people were cruel and systematically destroyed the towns they captured. Sidon fell to them, and was left a heap of ruins. Most of the inhabitants, however, succeeded in escaping by sea and taking refuge in Tyre. This influx of people with industrial secrets and particular knowledge of the sea proved of great benefit to Tyre, which entered into a period of remarkable economic expansion.

86

When peace returned to the region a new period of prosperity began for the Phoenician towns. Moreover, the weakening of Egypt's authority had left them independent, and none of the successors of Ramses the Great was capable of halting the country's decline.

An insight into Egypt's loss of prestige can be gained from the following story of Wen-Amon, who lived in the time of Ramses the Great and was a priest of the temple of Amon at Thebes. The pharaoh entrusted Wen-Amon with the very important mission of buying cedar for Amon-Ra's new ship. The powerful god was entitled to one new ship a year at the very least. However, the high priest Herihor, who was in charge of the depleted royal treasury, gave Wen-Amon a very limited sum of money for the purchase of the timber. So it was with a light pocket but a heart filled with gladness that Wen-Amon set forth on his journey, bearing letters of introduction to the authorities of the Delta and to Zecher-Baal, King of Gebal. He carried a small model of the god Amon on his person, to watch over him during his long journey.

Wen-Amon sailed from the Delta aboard a Phoenician ship, being given—as was customary for high official travelers even in those days—the full V.I.P. treatment. He reached Gebal safely, except that he was robbed of all his money on the way, at a place called Tjeker (a name which often appears in Egyptian records). As the King of Tjeker made no attempt to find the thief, Wen-Amon stole thirty pieces of silver before continuing his journey. News of his theft reached Gebal, and on his arrival Wen-Amon was told his presence was undesirable. However, he managed to obtain temporary permission to stay, although Zecher-Baal refused to receive him. The King wanted to keep on the right side of the neighboring kingdom of Tjeker, but at the same time did not want to miss a good piece of business.

At the end of a month Wen-Amon, greatly lamenting his misfortunes, was about to return in despair to Egypt when the King of Gebal sent for him. According to the account given by Wen-Amon a kind of miracle had occurred at court. A young visionary had gone into a trance and cried: "Bring the god here! Bring the messenger bearing his image!" It is more likely that the prospects of a business deal had greater attraction for the King than the god's image. But some excuse was necessary both for detaining the pharaoh's envoy and reassuring the King of Tjeker. There seems little doubt that Zecher-Baal was a shrewd businessman, possibly gifted with a keen sense of humor.

Wen-Amon, having no means to pay for the ship timber,

Amulet

reminded Zecher-Baal that his father, and his father before him, had sent timber for Amon-Ra's ship. The King replied that such was indeed the case—and that he would do the same, if adequately paid for the timber. In the end, Zecher-Baal accepted a deposit from Wen-Amon (the thirty pieces of silver stolen at Tjeker) and in return supplied some timber, enough to make the keel and the masts of the ship. The rest would be sent when the price was brought from Egypt by a messenger. Zecher-Baal drew up a list of the goods he required in exchange for his timber, and an impressive list it was: four gold vases and one smaller, five silver jars, ten rolls of linen (best quality), ten rolls of cloth from Upper Egypt, five hundred rolls of papyrus, five hundred animal skins, five hundred coils of hemp, twenty sacks of beans and thirty crates of dried fish. Zecher-Baal was well aware that the priests of Amon were rich and possessed all these things, which he greatly needed. They were duly sent from Egypt, and Zecher-Baal at once ordered three hundred men to the forests to cut down the timber for Amon-Ra's ship. And some weeks later Wen-Amon sailed from Gebal with the cargo, his mission at last accomplished.

It is clear from this account recorded by Wen-Amon that times had certainly changed since the envoys of Tuthmosis III had been received with great pomp and ceremony by the kings of Phoenicia. Zecher-Baal had not only demanded payment, he had shown his scorn of Egypt. While prepared to do business with the pharaoh's envoy, being fully aware of the material advantages of continuing to trade with Egypt, the King of Gebal negotiated from a position of strength and showed he had little fear of the pharaoh's wrath. The decline of Egyptian power was a time of the rise of the Phoenicians', whose ports were the gates to the Mediterranean.

Phoenician ship

Ship of Tarshish

Chapter 10

THE HOLLANDERS OF ANTIQUITY

The richest and most powerful of the city-kingdoms of Phoenicia were Tyre and Sidon, while Gebal had the prestige of being the oldest. The early Phoenicians had settled along the coast at places where a narrow neck of land gave them greater safety against attack and provided shelter for their ships, which they could usually moor under the lee of the peninsula. They soon realized, however, that this natural protection was not sufficient, and set about the construction of jetties and breakwaters. At Sidon, where there was a small bay on either side of the peninsula, the people built strong jetties and gave their town two safe harbors.

Some Greek writers—Tatius was one—believed that the people of Sidon had dug a canal across the small peninsula to connect their two harbors. But archaeologists have not discovered any confirmation of this, though excavations have revealed remains of sea walls which must have been large and well built. Indeed, Sidon was regarded in antiquity as the greatest and most important of the Phoenician ports. The Bible refers to it as "the eldest of Canaan," meaning the founder-city of the Phoenicians, and Homer calls all Phoenicians "Sidonians."

Sidon remained the chief port for trade and industry and had the largest fleet until it was captured and destroyed by the Philistines in 1209 B.C. Many of its inhabitants, however, managed to escape by sea to Tyre. This influx, mentioned in the previous chapter, was of great benefit to Tyre, whose rulers thenceforth gave themselves the title of King of the Sidonians. This proud addition was not intended as a tribute to the older

89

town but as a sign of superiority, for Tyre had always been envious of Sidon. Throughout Sidon's existence there is no evidence that Tyre ever once went to its aid when it was in need.

Tyre was founded on a small rocky headland which had only a narrow strip of ground at its base. On the north side was a little bay with a rocky islet at its entrance. As the settlement grew, more space became necessary, and this was obtained to seaward. There was a string of eight islets just offshore. The channel between the two largest was filled in, and a new town was built on the island so created. But this, too, became over-populated. The houses stood packed together and—wrote Strabo, the Roman geographer—were three and often four

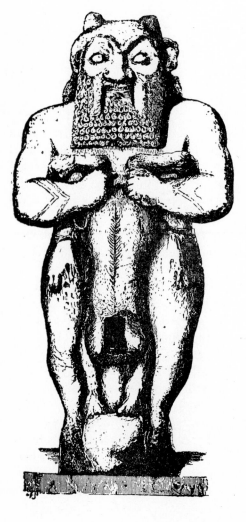

Melkart, "The King of the City," one of the principal deities of Tyre. His physical strength has led to comparisons with Hercules

stories high. Tyre was in urgent need of an "overspill," and the solution adopted was an astonishing one for the time—land was wrested from the sea between the island and the rocky headland by pouring in a vast amount of stones and rubbish. It can thus be said that the Phoenicians preceded the Hollanders in the making of polders by some three thousand years. The scale of reclamation work was admittedly very much smaller, but the means and techniques must have been much less adequate.

During the long period of building up and draining this new ground, Tyre had to withstand a number of enemy attacks. The ramparts that had been built on the landward side of the original settlement were not strong enough to hold off an enemy for long. The island town was a very different matter, and its walls could have stood up to bombardment if ships had been equipped with siege engines at that time. Moreover, the Tyrian fleet was continually being increased, and it enabled the town to hold out against Nebuchadnezzar, King of Babylonia, for thirteen years—the only one of the towns along the Phoenician seaboard to put up so stubborn a resistance to the all-conquering monarch. But then the large warehouses of Tyre were well stocked with food, and the powerful fleet kept sea communications open almost continually throughout the siege, so that supplies were maintained and Tyre could have defied the enemy indefinitely from behind its solid ramparts.

Two more centuries passed before Tyre fell to an assailant, and then only to the military genius of Alexander. He attacked by land and sea, building a causeway over the strip of water that divided the island town from the mainland, and so enabling his army to reach the very walls of Tyre.

Before that happened, however, Tyre had a very long and eventful history.

The island town lacked a good harbor in the early days, and one was essential for the little kingdom to expand its trade. The remaining rocky islets to the west formed a natural breakwater, but the small bay on the north of the headland was exposed and ships at anchor were frequently buffeted by onshore winds. So the Tyrians built two parallel breakwaters 240 yards long and 38 yards apart, extending out to sea from the northern tip of the island to a rock east of the bay. They were made from blocks of hard stone. The inner breakwater was more than 30 feet wide and was used as a jetty. There was room for hundreds of their ships in this sheltered anchorage, but when the sea was rough and the wind was blowing from the north it was almost impossible for them to put to sea by this Sidonian

91

access, as the opening was called because it faced Sidon, to the north. So the Tyrians built another harbor on the south side of their island, using much the same methods as for the first but on a larger scale. A breakwater nearly two miles in length stretched from a rock south of the island toward the shore, and a short jetty went from the rock to the southern tip of the island, thus making a large expanse of sheltered water where many hundreds of ships could moor and be loaded and unloaded. When this south-facing harbor (called the Egyptian access) was completed, the engineers began an even bolder undertaking; a wide canal was dug across the island to join the two harbors, thus enabling ships to pass from one to the other without sailing around the island.

Imagine the animated everyday scene in the heart of the city-kingdom when this wide canal was in full use, with ships of many kinds passing along it—sleek ships built for speed, with curved stem and stern, squat fishing boats, warships with a pointed ram, royal sailing barges, Tarshish ships with goods from many lands heaped on their decks, ferryboats and rafts of all sorts. This diversity of craft on the grand canal of Tyre must have given the city an atmosphere not unlike that of modern Venice. And watching over it all, from his temple on the highest point of the island realm, was the great god Melkart.

The cargoes loaded in these harbors were the products of Phoenician artisans and craftsmen, apart from the quantities of ship timber, most of which went to Egypt. Much of the cargoes were wooden objects and tools, for the forests were an almost inexhaustible supply of excellent raw material, and the Phoenicians had become skillful at working in wood. But they exported various other specialties too, glassware, for instance. Phoenician glass, especially that of Sidon, was renowned for its quality. The Egyptians had known glass long before the Phoenicians appeared on the scene, but it was not transparent. There are several stories about the invention of glass. According to Pliny, the crew of a Phoenician ship bound for Sidon with a cargo of niter landed on a deserted beach to cook themselves a meal. Having lit a fire, they looked around for some boulders or large stones on which to stand their cooking pots, but could find none on the sandy beach. So they fetched some blocks of niter from the ship and placed them around the fire. While the sailors were eating, the heat melted the niter and it oozed into the fine sand. When they began clearing up, they found an entirely new substance, firm and transparent. Whether this tale be fact or fiction, it is well known that many of man's

92

Gold bracelets

discoveries have been due to some lucky chance; and there was no such thing as a patent in ancient times. . . .

In any case, the Phoenicians were never inventors or creators, but improved on the discoveries and original ideas of others. They knew there was more wealth to be gained that way, and they were the experts at finding markets and selling what people required. The Tyrians became specialists in the glass industry, producing drinking bowls, plates and vases, all of which were much sought after on the markets of the ancient world. Phoenician glassware was famous for its thinness and graceful shapes; some objects were given the form of fish or slender plants, and even brightly colored glass was produced. Another specialty, greatly appreciated by the ladies, were glass beads with a glittering gem inside.

Colored glass became a common currency for trading transactions in underdeveloped regions. The Phoenicians were adept at arousing the curiosity and acquisitiveness of

93

primitive peoples, and the desires of women for personal ornaments. And they quite saw the vast marketing possibilities existing in more civilized lands in the decoration of temples and sanctuaries and even private dwellings. It is not difficult to imagine the huge profits the Phoenicians must have made from an industry for which the raw materials cost so little.

The Phoenicians worked in metal and exported these products too. But to obtain raw materials—copper and tin—their ships had to make very long voyages, to Spain, northwest France or even southwest England. Nevertheless, they sold vast quantities of copper and brass work in all the eastern Mediterranean lands. Its reputation was such that King Solomon sent for a Tyrian metalworker to decorate the Temple. This artisan's name was Hiram; his father was a Tyrian and his mother a Hebrew.

"...he was filled with wisdom, and understanding, and cunning to work all works in brass. And he came to King Solomon, and wrought all his work." (I Kings 7:14.) And again: he was "skillful to work in gold and in silver, in brass, in iron, in stone, and in timber, in purple, in blue, and in fine linen, and in crimson; also to grave any manner of graving, and to find out every device..." (II Chronicles 2:14.) Hiram was also an architect and a mason as well as engraver and decorator —a sort of Leonardo da Vinci of the Tyrian "classic" period.

Some of the work done by Phoenician bronzesmiths and coppersmiths would raise problems for artisans today. The two bronze pillars erected in the Temple by Hiram are described in the Old Testament.

"He cast two pillars of brass, of eighteen cubits high apiece: and a line of twelve cubits did compass either of them about. And he made two chapiters of molten brass, to set upon the tops of the pillars: the height of the one chapiter was five cubits, and the height of the other chapiter was five cubits:

"And nets of checker work, and wreaths of chain work, for the chapiters which were upon the top of the pillars; seven for the one chapiter, and seven for the other chapiter. And he made the pillars, and two rows round about upon the one network, to cover the chapiters that were upon the top, with pomegranates: and so did he for the other chapiter.

"And the chapiters that were upon the top of the pillars were of lily work in the porch, four cubits. And the chapiters upon the two pillars had pomegranates also above, over against the belly which was by the network: and the pomegranates were two hundred in rows round about upon the other chapiter.

"And he set up the pillars in the porch of the temple: and he set up the right pillar, and called the name thereof Jachin; and he set up the left pillar, and called the name thereof Boaz. And upon the top of the pillars was lily work; so was the work of the pillars finished." (I Kings 7:15-22.)

Each pillar was more than seventy-five feet high—an amazing work, even though it was not cast entirely in one piece. But the Altar was: "Moreover he made an altar of brass, twenty cubits the length thereof, and twenty cubits the breadth thereof, and ten cubits the height thereof. Also he made a molten sea of ten cubits from brim to brim, round in compass, and five cubits the height thereof; and a line of thirty cubits did compass it round about." (II Chronicles 4:1 and 2.)

The decoration of Solomon's Temple was a most ambitious undertaking, and the Hebrew chroniclers had every right to be proud of Hiram's origins.

Phoenician works of art were so highly thought of in ancient Greece that they were given as prizes at the Athenian games. Homer has Achilles give a chased silver bowl for the winner of a foot race: "It held ten measures, but was most remarkable for the beauty of the workmanship, which surpassed that of all others. Skillful craftsmen of Sidon had shaped and modeled it; then Phoenicians had brought it over the misty sea, displayed it in the ports . . ."

Yet despite their skill at working in metals and in glass, the Phoenicians had little originality. They absorbed other peoples' ideas—those of the Cretans, the Babylonians, and Egyptians—but it cannot be said that their art had any distinctive trends. On the other hand, they can be credited with considerable technological advance and great mastery of their materials.

Glassware and metalwork were by no means the sum of their products which they exported. The quality and different shades of color of Phoenician cloth and linen had a wide reputation. . . . When the gracious wife of Priam, King of Troy, sought favors from the goddess Athena, the gift she made was a splendid gown from Sidon.

PLATE 6

Phoenician ship of the Tarshish trade, thirteenth century B.C.

This model, designed by M. Pliner and built by M. I. Krupnik from a mural painting in a tomb at Thebes of the thirteenth century, shows Phoenician ships anchored in an Egyptian harbor. "For the King had at sea a navy of Tarshish with the navy of Hiram: once in three years came the navy of Tarshish, bringing gold and silver, ivory and apes, and peacocks. . . . And the navy also of Hiram, that brought gold from Ophir, brought in from Ophir a great plenty of almug trees and precious stones"— I Kings, 10:11 and 22.

There is a single mainsail, with gratings along the bulwarks to keep cargo in place and to ensure the safety of the crew in rough seas. Ships of this type sailed along the coasts of the Mediterranean and the Red Sea to reach the fabulous lands of Ophir and Tarshish. King Solomon had a marine base on the Red Sea, at Ezion-Geber, near Elat. This ship is very broad-beamed and deep in the hull, rigged with a wide mainsail and steered by two steering oars pivoting on the poop and worked by handles. Prow and stern are of the same shape and carved, with fishtail terminals. Normally, in this kind of ship, the cargo was carried in the waist and below decks.

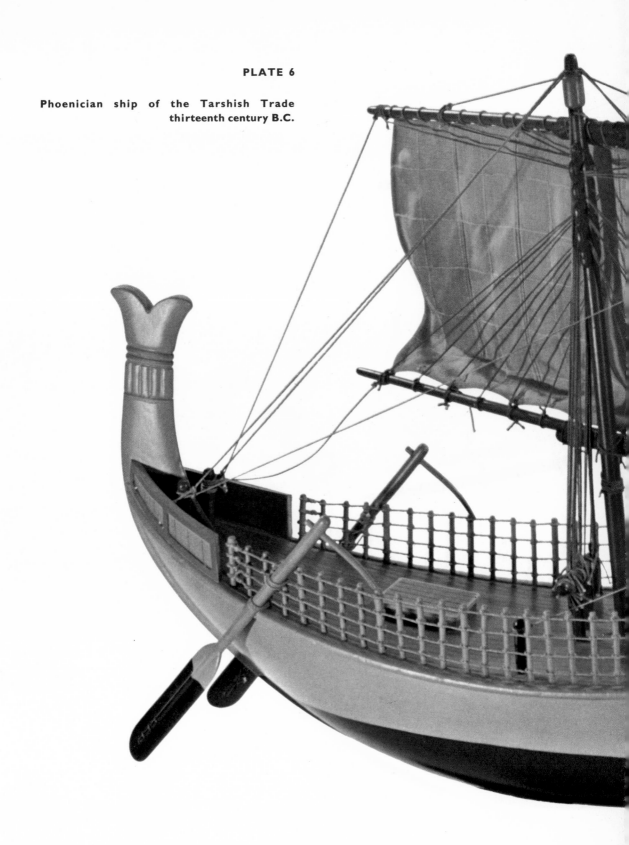

PLATE 6

Phoenician ship of the Tarshish Trade
thirteenth century B.C.

Phoenician coin

Chapter 11

PROSPERITY FROM THE SEA

According to the Greeks it was their hero Heracles who discovered the secret of making purple dye, although they admitted—with uncommon generosity toward trade competitors —that it happened on a Phoenician shore. The Greek story was that Heracles was walking on the beach at Tyre one day, accompanied by his dog and a local nymph called Tyros. Heracles had a reputation as a lady's man in addition to his other qualities of bravery and immense strength. He was said to have fathered more than three thousand children—no mean feat, especially in view of his many other exploits and the Twelve Labors he had to perform. In any case, there seems little doubt that his stroll along the beach with the pretty Tyrian nymph had some ulterior motive. But while his dog was nosing along the shore it came upon a shellfish, took a bite, and the victim's blood squirted over the dog's muzzle, giving it a dark red color that shone brightly in the sun. The nymph exclaimed in delight when she saw this fine new color, and said to Heracles: "I shan't love you until you've given me a gown of that color!" So the unfortunate Heracles set about gathering a quantity of the shellfish. He squeezed them and extracted enough purple

97

liquid to dye a gown. And when the nymph was given her purple gown she kept her part of the bargain in a most delightful manner.

The legend does not explain how Heracles caught the shellfish, which normally kept to the bottom of the sea, or how he made the dye and applied it to the gown. But the originators of the story, having a true Greek sense of proportion, probably considered that such details were best omitted . . . . Heracles had great strength but his mental capacities were in inverse ratio to it.

There may well have been more than a grain of truth in the story. Perhaps a few such shellfish were washed up, and local fishermen noticed that the rocks nearby were stained an unusual color. One thing is certain—purple dye was made by people who discovered these living shellfish, which were found in abundance off the eastern shores of the Mediterranean and particularly in the region of Tyre. The scientific name by which this shellfish is now known is *murex trunculus*. Fishermen caught it with long lines to which were attached baskets or pots containing bait such as frogs, worms, insects and seafood like shrimps; once the murex got into the pot it was trapped. In fact, the method was not unlike that of lobster catching. The murex, though, has a small pouch holding various fluids that it squirts to protect itself, in a similar manner to the cuttlefish. When caught, the murexes were winkled out of their shells, chopped up small, ground and put in a large lead container. Copper or iron ore was added, and the process of oxidation slightly changed the color of the pasty mixture. The container was then heated by steam and kept in the hot sunshine. By a judicious variation of these two forms of heating the contents, a dye of different color could be obtained—lemon, green, violet, red or purple. The last color necessitated a high temperature being maintained for ten days, and the contents had to be sifted many times to eliminate all remains of the murexes. The precious liquid then obtained was deep red.

The cloth or wool to be dyed was immersed in the liquid, sometimes two or three times, and then put to dry. This final step in the whole complicated process was of great importance, as the amount and degree of sunlight to which the material was exposed determined its color.

The people of Tyre discovered that purple dye could be obtained from another shellfish native to their shores (now known as the *purpura lapillum* or *buccinum*). This kind was found in shallow waters, which was an advantage, and gave a purple dye of a richer, brighter shade than the murex, but there were doubts as to whether its quality was as good. The Tyrians soon found, however, that material dipped in dye from murex and then in the other acquired a particularly fine shade of purple, deep and blackish, but which took on a brilliant dark red in the sun, lovely to the eye.

Tyrian purple never faded; the material remained rich and glowing in color until worn out. This explains why it was so widely sought after, and was found in Egypt, Assyria, and Babylonia, in Israel, Greece, and Rome. According to creditable Roman sources a length of silk dyed Tyrian purple and weighing about a pound cost, in A.D. 300, the equivalent of little short of $30,000!

In antiquity the price of purple cloth reached a fantastically high level. The merchants of Tyre would not have failed to exploit the fact that the color had become a sign of wealth and power, or to draw every advantage from the eternal desire of women to appear in the height of fashion.

It was always possible to tell where purple dye was being made, because of the horrible smell from the containers standing in the hot sun. Greek traders did not hide their disgust at the fetid odors on the Tyrian beaches, though it was a different matter when they discovered the secret and were able to make the dye themselves. Then they soon overcame their aversion and applied themselves to a task that, though obnoxious, earned huge profits.

Piles of empty shells can still be found along the coast between Sidon and Tyre. And it is not difficult to imagine what the smells must have been when hundreds of thousands of shellfish were rotting in the sun.

The smell was not the only handicap to the making of the dye. Each murex secreted only a few drops of the precious liquid. A great number were needed to obtain a relatively small amount of dye, so that before very long the supply became exhausted and the Tyrians had to seek their raw material on shores other than their own.

The wealth and prosperity of the Phoenicians were drawn from the sea itself, not just from its translucent depths. The deep blue Mediterranean was a constant invitation to the Tyrians. There are times when this inland sea is whipped up into a furious rage, but it soon recovers its serenity and the blue and green crystal-clear waters lap gently against the shores once again. The azure sea under a deep blue sky, with rarely a cloud to be seen, enchants the mind and is balm to the soul.

99

And when the sun goes down, leaving the sky streaked with colors from pink to purple, the night does not entirely cover the Mediterranean—a soft luminosity remains, so that full night already heralds the dawn. It is a beautiful sea, a wonderful sea, and there can be no surprise that the early seafarers should have set sail upon its waters with a light heart, confident of returning safely to port. The Mediterranean shores were the cradle of civilization, the sea was the common heritage of Cretans, Phoenicians, and Greeks, thus linked despite their different characteristics and dissimilar origins. And untold riches were waiting to be gathered by whoever became at home on these blue waters.

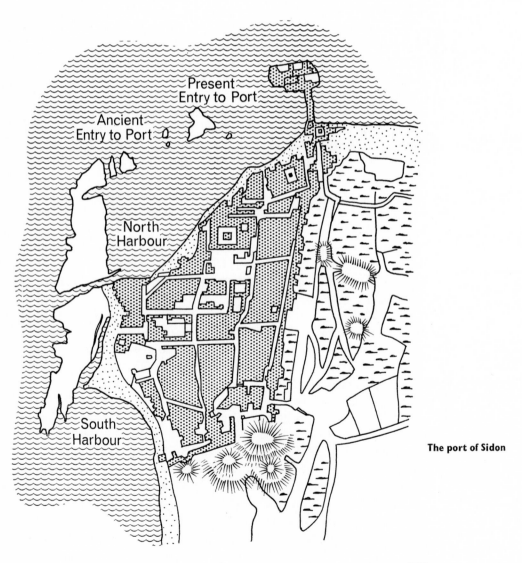

The port of Sidon

100

Akkadian seal

The Tyrians proved to be the cleverest at exploiting the limitless possibilities, making maximum use of their large fleet based at the port they had built so well. By maintaining a monopoly in the trading of many rare goods, they became the most successful merchant adventurers in antiquity. They were the first to think of lighting flares to help guide their ships into harbor on stormy nights. It is not certain whether they had coastal maps, though their sailors must have accumulated an extensive knowledge of land bearings and offshore reefs, sandbanks, currents and the like. Ptolemy the geographer is known to have had a forerunner in Marinus of Tyre, but hardly anything is known of Marinus' work.

Greek writers mistakenly attributed the scientific discovery of astronomy to the Phoenicians, who in fact learned of it from the Babylonians and adapted the knowledge to their practical needs, steering their ships at night by observations of the Pole Star and the Great Bear. The Phoenicians studied the tides and the prevailing winds, and they knew of the monsoons in the Indian Ocean long before the Greek merchant Hippalus wrote about them. Each new item of maritime information was of great help to all Phoenician seafarers, and in time they came to possess a vast knowledge of navigation—which they kept to themselves. King Solomon said that one of the four secrets of the universe was "the track made by a ship across the sea"; and the Phoenicians were well aware that the only means of discovering that track was to follow in the wake of the ship. An incident recounted by Strabo is highly indicative of how far Phoenician sea captains

101

would go in order to keep their maritime and trading secrets from foreign competitors:

"The Phoenicians plied this trade [tin from Cornwall] alone, keeping their route from Gades hidden from all men. When the Romans shadowed one of their skippers, in order to discover their marts, the skipper deliberately cast up his vessel on a sandbank. Having thus lured his pursuers to the destruction which he had likewise courted for himself, he saved his own life, and received back on public account the value of the cargo which he had sacrificed."

The Phoenicians had so many merits that there is no need to give them laurels to which they are not entitled. The pure sciences and all abstract thought held no interest for them, unless they could apply to their needs the knowledge gained by others. But they excelled in the art of negotiation, being endowed with limitless patience and much tolerance. At the

102

same time they were an energetic people, always ready for action, possessing great stamina and vigor. Their seamen had no hesitation in setting out on long voyages and venturing into unknown waters, sometimes being away for many months, even years—for more than three years in the case of the voyage around Africa.

They were essentially realists; questions which troubled other peoples in antiquity, such as life after death and what happened to a dead person's body, did not worry them unduly. Nor were they inspired by nature or the relationship between man and the gods. To judge by what little of their literature has survived, they had no tradition of any worth in this respect.

**Phoenician gem, showing
a Tyrean ship
and dolphins**

Chapter 12

TRADERS AND PIRATES

The eminent place held by the Phoenicians in the history of their time, when brute force was the only known law, was firmly based upon their trading empire. This is not to say they never took up arms when the situation demanded it, but they never waged an aggressive war or carried out mass slaughter such as usually accompanied the ferocious conquests of that age. It was by peaceful means, through the spread of trade and industry, that they built up their power—in much the same way as, many centuries later, the Republic of Venice, the Netherlands, Britain.... But it would be a mistake to conclude that the Phoenicians were pacifists who made a high ideal of diplomatic competition. Ideals of that kind had no interest for them. They succeeded in building up a great commercial empire, but without any preconceived plan or objective. It was the particular trading conditions prevailing, the necessity of acquiring supply bases for their ships on long voyages, the powerful urge to make large profits, the need to retain a good clientele and, especially, probity

105

in their trading—all that had gone to the making of the Phoenician empire.

Not content with marketing their own products, the
Phoenicians went into the slave trade. They bought their human
merchandise from warring people and then sold it in European,
African, and Asian countries which were in need of a labor
force. In this trade, as in all others, the Phoenicians maintained
a strict neutrality. It mattered little to them who were the
defeated people—these prisoners of war were just slaves to be
sold at a profit. The fortunes of war might change and a defeated
tribe become victors over their late conquerors; it was all the
same to the Phoenicians, who bought as slaves those who had
been victors in the past.

There were times, however, when this source of supply
dwindled to less than a trickle, and the Phoenicians then had
recourse to a much simpler and cheaper method. They attacked
ships and carried off passengers and crew into slavery. They also
raided coastal villages for the same purpose, thus setting a
precedent for the Barbary pirates centuries later.

Phoenician statuette

There was much demand from Eastern potentates for pretty
young women and girls, especially virgins, for their harems,
and the Phoenicians were practically the only slave traders able
to supply them. In this commercial activity the Phoenicians
maintained their high standards in the quality of their
merchandise. Tribes in the Caucasus sold their daughters for a
good price, but in Asia Minor, the Crimea, and Greece more
forcible means had to be employed. . . . The Phoenicians took no
personal interest in the young women and girls they procured.
Their religious cult with its numerous sacred prostitutes largely
sufficed in this respect. Besides, the higher market value of a
virgin was of greater interest to them than the pleasures of
ravishing her; as always with the Phoenicians, quality was what
mattered, worship of the golden calf was preferred to that of
beauty.

Herodotus believed that all the troubles of the world were
due to women. Of the Phoenicians, ravishers of women, he
wrote: "The crews of some Phoenician ships landed on the
shores of Argos, then the foremost of the Greek city-states, and
displayed their wares for five or six days. At the end of that
time, when they had sold most of their cargo, a large group of
women went down to make some purchases. The daughter of
King Inachos was among them. As they approached the ships
drawn up on the beach, the Phoenicians suddenly swept down
on them and, amid cries and shrieks, carried a good many off

106

to their ships, including the king's daughter, Io. The Phoenicians then shook out their sails and made towards Egypt."

The Phoenicians had probably been conducting themselves in a friendly manner while selling their wares, and there had seemed no danger in the women's going down to the shore without an escort. But then the close view of these graceful and beautiful women and girls—quite the equal of those of modern Greece—had given the traders a sudden idea. Concerted action was swiftly decided on and the whole operation carried out in a very short time—as one would expect from professionals. When armed men of the locality hurried to the shore, the ships and their captives were a long way out at sea.

According to Herodotus this kidnaping of King Inachos's daughter was the chief cause of the Trojan War. The Greeks were furious and took their revenge by carrying off Phoenician women—and women of other races, too. In fact, being men of good taste and discernment, they were not at all keen on Phoenician women. They much preferred those of Troy, who were pretty and graceful, besides having many hidden virtues.... But the Trojan men, far from being flattered by this preference of the Greeks, replied by capturing the beautiful Helen. The Greeks then assembled a large fleet, attacked and captured Troy and thoroughly plundered it. So the Persians took up arms, through "regional solidarity," and set out to avenge the Trojans.

Aristophanes made fun of this story, but Herodotus was being quite serious, and as an objective historian also gave the Phoenician version of the affair at Argos. The king's daughter Io had not been kidnaped—she had fallen in love with the captain of one of the Phoenician ships. All very natural, according to the Phoenicians. Then, realizing she was pregnant, Io left the town of her own accord and went away with her lover, not so much through shame as from fear of her father's wrath. Herodotus wisely refrained from favoring one or the other of the opposing versions—and indeed both are feasible.

Glazed Phoenician pottery

Homer, too, told a similar tale about Phoenicians (although he called them Canaanites).

Eumea was the son of the King of Syra, an island famous for its wine. "Men arrived from Canaan, fine seamen but hypocrites. In their ships were many wonderful things. There was a Canaanite woman in my father's house, a beautiful, slim woman, clever with her hands, and the crafty seamen led her astray."

They did this while she was "washing clothes near the ship" and in a manner "likely to win the hearts of sensitive women, even those with high morals."

This woman from Sidon was Eumea's wet nurse, and the King's son was "an intelligent child worth his weight in gold" to anyone who kidnaped him—which the Phoenicians, with the help of the wet nurse, were planning to do. They stayed on the island for a whole year. Then, having sold or bartered all their goods, they loaded their purchases into their ships and prepared to set sail. They sent a messenger to the King's palace to inform the Sidonian woman that the ships were about to sail. The messenger was also the bearer of a gold necklace set with amber, and while the King and his attendants were looking at this with great interest the Sidonian woman seized the child (and three cups of great value) and hurried down to . . .

> The much-vaunted harbor where lay
> The light ship of the Canaanites.
> They went aboard, and took us aboard too,
> Then put to sea, and Zeus caused a fair wind to blow.

However, the Greek gods could not allow such treachery and cruelty to go unpunished, and a week after the ship had sailed Artemis—goddess of justice and guardian of women's honor— killed the deceitful Sidonian with a well-directed arrow.

These tales and others like them give the impression that the Greeks had a low opinion of the Phoenicians, who were in fact often referred to as pirates. Had they really such a bad reputation in the ancient world? Or were such reports of them historical libels having their origins in causes still unknown to us? They probably contained a certain amount of truth, inasmuch as the Phoenicians did not always distinguish between honest trading and sharp practices, between fair dealing and piracy. They were not above swindling the simple and robbing the weak, but acted squarely with those whose strength and cunning were equal to their own. It must be admitted in their defense, however, that most of the time they were scrupulously honest

108

in their dealings; this enabled them to maintain good trade relations in many lands. If they had engaged in nothing but trickery and theft it would hardly have been possible for Herodotus to have written the following account of trading practices of the Carthaginians, the direct descendants of Tyrians.

> On arrival at a place they unload their goods and set them out near the water's edge in an attractive manner, then return to their ships and send up a smoke signal from the deck. When the people of the place see the smoke they go down to the shore, inspect the goods and leave an amount of gold which in their opinion represents the value. After they have gone away, the Carthaginians return to the shore, and if the amount of gold seems enough they take it and continue on their way. Otherwise they leave the gold and their goods untouched, and go back to their ships and wait. The people go down again and add to the gold, until the amount is acceptable to the Carthaginians. Neither party tries to cheat the other. The Carthaginians do not touch the gold while the amount is deemed insufficient. And the people do not touch the goods while the gold is still there.

As a historical source, Herodotus is interesting and reliable when he discards his chauvinism and writes objectively. If a Greek such as he shows the Phoenicians in a favorable light then we can be sure they were not just pirates, as was often insinuated.

Their merchandise was always of the best quality, and was known to be so the world over; their kings and merchants alike had every confidence in their wares and also in their trading methods. To carry off a few women was no great crime in the ancient world, and anyone could get away with a little trickery provided it was successful. But if the Phoenicians had constantly engaged in malpractices they would soon have lost the confidence of the peoples with whom they traded, and would have found themselves being refused entrance to harbors and warned off foreign shores. And the Phoenicians never tried to force their trade on any country. They penetrated by peaceful means, by persuasion and tact.

If the Greeks are to be believed, only the Phoenicians were pirates. But the real truth of the matter is that the Greeks themselves were not above piracy. Their country was very poor,

109

a condition difficult for such a talented and gifted people to support with equanimity. Poverty, then as always, drove people to improve their lot without being very particular about the means employed. The Phoenicians were known to be wealthy traders whose ships were laden with riches—and which often sailed close to Greek islands, putting in at night to some haven or sheltered creek, where the crews went ashore. What temptation for the local inhabitants! It was surely only logical for the idea of pillaging the ships to enter their heads. The marvelous cargoes within their reach would make life so much easier. The rocky coastline with its many offshore reefs gave the Greeks natural cover, and their sudden attacks after nightfall often took the Phoenicians by surprise, despite the latter's precautions. At the time of the Trojan War, Greek sailors were killing and plundering shamelessly instead of engaging in honest trading. They had little to sell, anyway. The sea has always been an open highway, without limits or defined frontiers, accessible to all adventurers, and without police to keep order and give protection.

Wealth usually arouses envy, and the Phoenicians were very rich. As their trading empire grew and their wealth increased, so the Greeks became bolder and more active in their piracy. It is an accepted idea the world over that the poor want to

110

become rich and the rich to be even richer. A state of open warfare existed between a merchant sea power and organized pirates, for the first time in history. There can be no doubt that piracy was then regarded as a profession, a branch of economic activity that brought important revenues to Greece. The seaways used by the Phoenicians necessarily passed between the Greek islands and close to the Greek mainland, so that the movements of Phoenician shipping were always known to the corsairs. They had a well-organized center on the island of Delos, which became internationally known as a slave market. Members of captured crews brought good prices, but much higher sums were obtained for Phoenician merchants by ransoming them.

The defensive measures taken by the Phoenicians included the building of fortified bases along their sea routes. These served as warehouses and trading posts, but were chiefly to give shelter to their ships. Watchtowers were built, and the guards gave warning of the approach of corsairs by making smoke fires in daytime, by lighting flares at night. The invention of lighthouses was probably due more to fear of pirates than to a desire to aid navigation. Be that as it may, the Tyrians were the first to develop the idea by building two slim lighthouses at the entrance to their harbor, though in those days the lighthouse had the dual purpose of aiding ships to avoid rocks and sandbanks and helping them to escape from pirates.

The Phoenicians became more daring as they accumulated experience, and were the first mariners to sail throughout the night, taking the stars as their guide. The normal practice had been to put in at nightfall, and this had given pirate ships their opportunity. But necessity drove the Phoenicians to discover means of continuing safely on their course. Moreover, they became the first to sail the open sea, instead of keeping to coastal waters or proceeding from island to island.

The Phoenicians accepted the inevitable risks at sea, but did their utmost to avoid or reduce the dangers. So it is not surprising, therefore, that they engaged at times in pursuits similar to those from which they suffered at the hands of the Greeks. Their chief aim was always to make the maximum profit in the best conditions and to avoid losses. They can hardly be blamed for sometimes enticing a few pretty women aboard their ships—they were so much engrossed in business affairs that the women were seen simply as good, negotiable merchandise. The Phoenicians were opportunists and seized any occasion to make something on the side.

111

When applied to foreigners the term "pirate" was meant as an insult by the Greeks, but when used among themselves it had a quite different significance. Homer often wrote it to describe a bold man who took a chance—at sea, of course. Those who engaged in piracy were regarded as heroes if they belonged to a Greek tribe. Their exploits were worthy of admiration and served to measure the importance and value of Homer's heroes. To amass riches by despoiling others seemed very natural; as the victims were not Greeks, they were of no importance. And as these somewhat cruel acts occurred far from home there was little point in bothering about them. Yet could not the Greek hero Achilles rightly be called a pirate? And what was the cunning Odysseus if not one? But to the Greeks his acts of piracy—more than seventy-seven of them—were symbolic of his daring and strength, cunning and wisdom. A pirate was a base individual only when a Phoenician, an Etruscan, or a Lydian; then piracy became reprehensible, an unpardonable crime.

To the Greeks, Jason and the Argonauts were great and intrepid heroes. To the people around the Black Sea, they were unscrupulous buccaneers. It was much like the opposing outlook of the English and Spanish with regard to Drake, Hawkins and company. Profitable attacks on foreign shipping by Greeks were regarded with favor at home, but attacks of the same nature on Greek ships were considered acts of aggression. So it would seem obvious that all adverse accounts and descriptions of the Phoenicians in ancient Greek literature should be treated with reserve.

Greek warship copied from Phoenician type

PLATE 7

Phoenician ship of the eighth century B.C.

This model, designed by Dr. Sotas and built by M. I. Krupnik, is based on an Assyrian bas-relief on the walls of the palace of King Sargon, who was famed for his mania for building palaces and temples, thus necessitating the import of building timber which is scarcely to be had in Mesopotamia. The relief on the palace walls shows beams of timber either stacked on the decks of ships or towed behind them in rafts. Ships of this kind are called *hippos*, from the Greek word for horse, because they always had a horse's head on the prow, though the sternpost was carved to represent a fishtail. There is a square sail amidships and ten oars on a side. The ship is steered by double steering oars, not pivoted but passing through the hull low down, on either side of the sternpost. There is a crow's nest for the lookout. The hull is exceptionally solid in construction. The Greek writer Strabo said that ships of this type were still in use in the first century of the Christian era. The Phoenicians used them for really long voyages, as far afield as Cornwall and perhaps other western promontories of Britain, and even to the coasts of the Baltic. This would explain the surprising resemblance in design between the *hippos* and the seagoing boats which were the ancestors of the Viking ships.

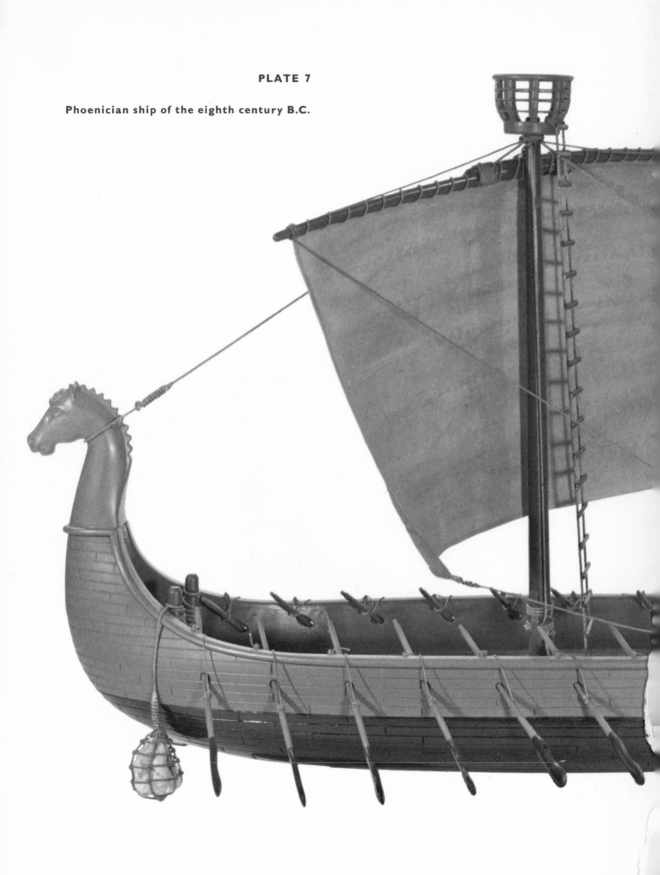

PLATE 7

Phoenician ship of the eighth century B.C.

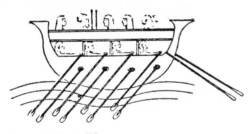

Cargo ship from Sidon

Chapter 13

FROM TYRE TO GIBRALTAR

The rich and powerful kingdom of Tyre had a veritable monopoly of trade with Egypt. Tyrians were allowed to establish trading posts on Egyptian soil and were even permitted to reside at Thebes—the only foreigners to receive such permission —and to build their own quarters there. They were also allowed to practice their own religious rites. The favored position of the Tyrians enabled them to make huge profits, which in turn permitted them to increase the size of their merchant fleet. Tyrian ships were better built, speedier and more seaworthy than those of any other people, and their crews were experienced sailors who loved the sea and regarded it as their domain, an immense and beneficial domain. They knew all its moods and changes. They had learned everything about it of use to them, and had a close affinity with it. They had learned to calculate distances, and to navigate by the stars. So a time came when they felt ready for "the great adventure"—to seek new markets, establish trading posts on distant shores, in a word to sail westward into the unknown.

The Phoenicians were as intrepid in some matters as they were prudent in others. For a long time they were coastal sailors, or at least never ventured out of sight of land. Cyprus was their first "overseas" objective. On a clear day its dark outline was visible from Tyre or Sidon, as it was little more than fifty miles distant. The Tyrians established several trading posts on this lovely island, where there were many copper and iron mines. Precious stones, bright red and yellow, were found there too. Delicious fruit abounded, and the island was renowned for

113

its flowers, especially roses. The Greeks had every reason for calling it "the scented land."

The grapes that grew on Cyprus were large and juicy. Even in those times the island was famous for its wine, which then as now had a strong body and rejoiced the heart. The mountain slopes were covered with pine and cypress, like Crete, and provided excellent ship timber. Cypriot girls were reputed to be charming and most seductive, which was probably the reason for the island's having a Garden of Venus. A temple to the goddess of love (the Greek Aphrodite, or Astarte) stood in a splendid garden in the ancient town of Paphos. It was visited by people from all parts of the eastern Mediterranean, for the goddess Aphrodite-Astarte was known to possess great powers, and a new town grew up in the vicinity to cater to and draw profit from this flourishing tourist trade.

There is much evidence of Phoenician presence on Cyprus, but it should not be inferred that the Phoenicians occupied the island. Unlike the Greeks, they never conquered foreign lands, but were satisfied with establishing trading posts and consolidating trade relations. They had bases on Cyprus at Idalion, Kitaion and Tamissos, and at a few other places where they imported their own goods and exported those of the Cypriots. Although the Phoenicians were responsible for much of the economic development of Cyprus and influenced the religious cults, the island remained essentially Greek.

The Phoenicians next established bases in Cilicia, on the coast of Asia Minor north of Cyprus. But they made no effort to enter into contact with the peoples to the west, in Lycia and Caria, for these were poor countries whose inhabitants had little to sell or means for purchasing. The Phoenicians thus approached the Aegean, coming first to Rhodes; finding that this fertile and flourishing island had good, natural harbors, they built bases at Gelissos and Camiros. The position of Rhodes was a great attraction for the Phoenicians, and they endeavored to implant themselves on the island. For several generations, it was called "the Phoenician" by the Greeks, because of the number of buildings, harbors and markets constructed by the Tyrians. The chief of the colony at Camiros was said to be a relative of the King of Tyre.

It is not known for certain when and by whom the famous Colossus of Rhodes was built, though we can be sure that Phoenician ships sailed between its straddled legs. From Rhodes the many islands of the Aegean were within easy reach of the Phoenician ships, and the urge to prospect new markets was

114

probably the reason the Tyrians did not settle permanently on Rhodes. This lovely, fertile island was later conquered by the Carians, and then by Achaeans.

By way of the island of Carpathos the Phoenicians reached Crete, and thence the Cyclades, trading from one island to another, and later exporting their produce farther afield—marble from Paros, pyrites from Lemnos and Samothrace, sulphur from Melos. They exploited the gold mines on Thasos, where they established colonies to this end. According to Herodotus, they "shifted a whole mountain to find gold." Phoenician ships carried to Egypt fruit from Naxos, wheat from Syros and Samos, and wine from Lemnos and other islands. The Egyptians were fond of wine; the Greeks and Phoenicians, too, for that matter. There were many wineshops in the ports of Sidon and Tyre, and they were usually busy with sailors and workers who came for a drink, since it was not dear.

The Phoenicians consolidated their trade among the islands of the Aegean, paying for the raw materials and agricultural produce with manufactured goods. They established such strong connections that the Greek historian Thucydides—usually a reliable source—wrote that "it was chiefly the inhabitants of the islands who engaged in robbery—Carians and Phoenicians who had settled on most of the islands." But Phoenicians never actually resided permanently on any of the Aegean islands. And Thucydides in fact wrote at a later point in the same chapter: "The proof is . . . when the Athenians cleared up Delos and opened the graves of those killed in the war [of the Peloponnese], they found that more than half were Carians. They recognized them as such by the weapons buried with them and by the manner of their burial, which is still carried out in their own country."

Thucydides' "proof" is therefore not valid. The Phoenicians certainly exercised considerable influence over the islanders, but never settled among them.

In the course of their trading activities in the Aegean, the Tyrians were constantly searching for new supplies of shellfish for making purple dye, the product that was more essential even than gold or precious stones. The murex had become rare along the Tyrian shores. They eventually found a supply not far from the island of Cythera, which they had reached from Crete. The dye obtained from this shellfish was of inferior quality, but nevertheless purple.

Cythera was an excellent base for the Phoenicians, who built depots there and even repair yards for their ships. They also

115

introduced their religious cult to the island, but whereas they had set up temples to Melkart on several other islands, they built only a temple to Venus on Cythera. It seems that wherever the Phoenicians wished to settle permanently they built temples to the Goddess of Love. Several were built on the islands of Cythera and Cyprus, and the cult was later adopted by the Greeks.

The garden of Astarte

The description given by Herodotus of the cult as practiced on Cythera and Cyprus is evidence enough of its popularity in the ancient world. Every young woman was supposed to go at least once in her life to make sacrifice to the Goddess of Love (Astarte to the Babylonians, Aphrodite to the Cypriots and Greeks). It was a simple process. A group of women sat and waited in the gardens of the temple for a man to choose among them. He would invite one of them to the sacrifice by tossing her a coin. The cult forbade such invitation to be refused, nor were women allowed to leave the Garden of Venus without having given themselves to the goddess at least once. Herodotus, with his sly humor, commented that young and pretty women were soon free to leave but that their less fortunate sisters, especially those with some infirmity, might have to wait years for their "liberator." Virgins as well as married women had to offer themselves to the Goddess of Love and Fertility, through the intermediary of an anonymous male. And since the acolytes of the Goddess had not necessarily to belong to the weaker sex, it was hardly surprising that such great numbers of pilgrims were attracted to the sacred islands.

In spite of its proximity to the Aegean Sea, the Black Sea does not appear to have been frequented by the Phoenicians.

116

It had a bad reputation, and the peoples around its shores were said to be cruel and warlike. The honor of the effective discovery of the Black Sea was therefore left to the Greeks.

Nor do the Phoenicians seem to have penetrated the Adriatic; no evidence of them has been found on the east coast of Italy. If they did sail along that coast they very likely considered it poor and unwelcoming, lacking harbors and peopled by backward and warlike tribes—not at all an interesting proposition to the commercially minded and peace-loving Phoenicians.

But to the west it was a different matter. Fabulous lands containing countless treasures were said to exist in the distant West. Set course to the West then! The African coast of the Mediterranean appeared a more hospitable shore to follow than the northern. The peoples inhabiting it were more peaceful and more inclined to barter their products. Tyre was then at the height of its power and dominated the commerce of the Levant, so the search for the route to the West, to the lands of tin, copper, silver and gold, was undertaken with great assurance— but with prudence too. A hasty advance could mean great losses, possibly the ruin of the mother city. The Phoenicians had to bear in mind their relatively small manpower, and their eccentric position at the extreme end of the Mediterranean. So they advanced by stages along the coast of Africa, first founding Utica, a little to the west of present-day Tunis. Utica, probably the earliest colony in the real sense of the word, soon became a prosperous town and an important base for the Phoenicians. Other settlements followed, east and west of Utica, the largest being Leptis-Magna, Hadrumetum, Hippo-Diarrhytus, and Hippo-Regius.

The Phoenicians had a remarkably keen eye for choosing a base. The proof is the fact that other peoples later built cities on the ruins of the Phoenician colonies, and these sites are today

**Phoenician
vases**

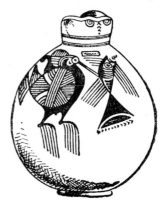

117

known as Sousse, Bizerte, Bône. In ancient times the hinterland was very fertile. North Africa, particularly Tunisia, was the granary of Rome for hundreds of years. The Phoenicians found iron ore in the hills and, even more important, salt flats by the sea. The city of Utica remained prosperous for many centuries, retaining her maritime and commercial importance even after the rise of Carthage.

From Utica the Phoenicians thrust across to western Sicily, and they soon realized that once they had established bases on the south and west coasts of this island they would control the southern Mediterranean. Any foreign ships wanting to proceed farther west would have to seek their permission, which meant paying sea tribute. Their experienced captains quickly discovered the most sheltered and easily defensible harbors. The first trading post was established at Hippo-Panhormos (present-day Palermo, still the most important port in Sicily). Then the Phoenicians installed themselves at Motya, took possession of Soloeis, and built temples at Eryx and Segesta, up in the mountains—not so much for religious purposes as because these sites were excellent observation posts over a wide expanse of sea.

The Phoenicians turned their attention to the smaller islands between Sicily and North Africa. Melita (Malta) was found to be barren but to have a splendid natural harbor, one of the best in the whole Mediterranean region. Cosseiros (Pantellaria), Lampas (Lampedusa), and Gaulos (Gozo) were equally barren and lacking in natural resources, but bases were established on each island because of its position on what had become an important sea route for the Phoenicians, especially in view of their objective in the West.

They established themselves firmly in Sicily and, although the Greeks tried to eject them by every warlike means, they succeeded in maintaining their positions. These traders fought hard and obstinately when their vital interests were at stake. Some historians have objected that the Phoenicians never actually settled in Sicily, yet there is the testimony of Thucydides, a sound Greek authority:

"The Phoenicians had establishments all round Sicily," he wrote. "They fortified the rocks along the shore and took possession of the small islands nearby, for the needs of their trade with the Sicilians. But when the Greeks began arriving in large numbers from across the sea they abandoned most of their settlements and concentrated at Motya, Soloeis, and Panhormos, near Elymi, partly because they trusted in the alliance they had made with the people of Elymi and partly

118

**Phoenician coin with
image of ship**

because the sea route to Karchedon was the shortest from there.
Such were the barbarians who dwelt in Sicily and such were
their ways of colonizing."

It can now be asserted that the Phoenicians were established
in Sicily before the Greeks, and that their settlements were taken
over by the Carthaginians, who stubbornly carried on merciless
and bloody warfare for hundreds of years against the Greeks—
whose colonies were chiefly on the east of the island.

From their bases on Sicily the Phoenicians colonized the
southwest of Sardinia, where they exploited the copper mines

119

and lead mines. But this was the limit of their penetration to the north, for there they were approaching areas controlled by the Etruscans. The origins of these people are still something of a mystery. It is not certain whether they were natives of Italy or immigrants from Asia Minor. In any case they built a powerful fleet and maintained a local thalassocracy. They and the Phoenicians were natural allies for several centuries, first against the Greeks, then against the Romans. There was another reason for remaining in the south. The natives of Sardinia had a reputation as hardy and cruel warriors, so the prudent Phoenicians avoided clashing with them, by limiting their bases to the southwest of the island. These bases were part of their chain of control of the southern Mediterranean.

There can be no doubt that the Phoenician objective in the West was Spain. The arguments of "Phoenicomanians" that Massilia (Marseilles) was founded by the Phoenicians will not stand close examination. Some etymologists seem to think that their fervor can prove anything. The name Massilia, they argue, is derived from the Canaan "Messilah"—so Marseilles must have been founded by Phoenicians! But no evidence of their presence has been discovered in that area, and the generally accepted theory is that Massilia, like Monaco, was founded by Greeks. The Phoenicians left those northern shores of the Mediterranean to the Greeks to explore and occupy, for they had no need of bases in that direction. Their next objective was farther west, the Balearics, and when they had occupied those islands their line of bases from Tyre to Gibraltar was complete.

Ship of Tarshish

Chapter 14

TARSHISH, THE ELDORADO IN THE WEST

So the way to the West was open, and the ancient world was on the verge of its greatest and boldest adventure. Columbus was still two thousand five hundred years in the future when the Phoenician seamen dared to break out of the hitherto enclosed world of their inner sea.

It was a bold venture for them, to sail forth into the rough gray seas beyond their own familiar horizon. But this unexplored region exerted a strong fascination. What new peoples might be found, what new lands opened up for trading? Here is the key to the voyages of these ever-ranging seamen. Curiosity led them on, the immensity of the empty, unknown sea was an attraction, but over and above was the desire to expand their sphere of trading. Especially, there was the craving for gold.

Their imagination had been stirred by tales of Tarshish (Tartessus), which was said to abound in copper and tin; river-beds were rich in silver, and every stone, every rock that was cracked open revealed its silver treasure. But Tarshish was above all the land of gold. Gold, whose luster reflected the glory of the sun, was the symbol of wealth and roused in man the desire for power and dominion. All down the ages men have felt the mysterious and contagious lure of gold. They have pledged their souls, given their lives for this cold, shining metal, and many are the legends woven round it. The sole object of Jason's voyage was to seize the Golden Fleece. The love of gold brought nothing but misery to Midas, King of Phrygia. Great wealth was at the source of all the ills that befell Croesus, King of Lydia.

121

In all parts of the world, legends abound of the fascinating, magnetic power of the king of metals; and at all times men have known of its evil, destructive power—ever since the children of Israel worshiped the golden calf. Neither the icy cold of Alaska nor the tropical heat of Africa has deterred men from their search for gold.

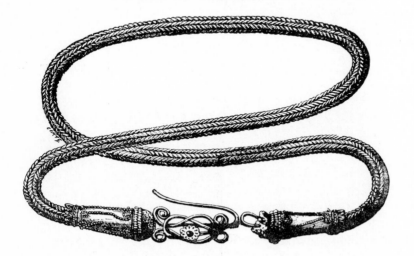

Necklace from Tyre

The history of gold is to some extent the history of man. Throughout the centuries, writers and philosophers have denounced the evils of gold, stressing its devilish, destructive power. Gold indeed corrupts the soul, or so many think. Moralists claim that they can judge character by the way a person reacts to the temptation of gold. Bacon described gold as the touchstone of man's purity. Yet the influence of gold is not entirely negative. The dark side of its reputation has probably been stressed because of man's tendency to report on the bad side of human activities. The quest for this precious metal has certainly brought in its train much cruelty and has tempted many into devious ways, but it should not be forgotten that gold has played a part in the progress of civilization, that countries have been developed and natural disasters overcome with its aid. Gold and silver have contributed to raise the standard of living. Towns have been built, agriculture developed and continents discovered because of it. This positive function of gold is natural enough, but no one has yet explained satisfactorily why gold was adopted as a standard value for trading. Whatever the reason, it has become a formidable and powerful driving force.

The Phoenicians sought as much information as they could about Tarshish. The Mediterranean people excelled themselves

122

in relating horrifying stories of the seas beyond Gibraltar. They were hostile waters, stretching away to infinity, that would engulf any who ventured on them. They were shrouded in dank mists and terrifying gloom, unlike the clear and reassuring inner sea. All sailors knew some tale or legend that would strike terror into people's hearts. But there were other, less dramatic tales, holding hope of wealth and happiness in faraway lands. At that particular period, about the middle of the Bronze Age, the Phoenicians would certainly have heard of the mysterious metal, tin, which had the property of changing copper into a hard, malleable metal. They had already founded copper industries at Tyre, Sidon, Gebal, and at nearby colonies. They probably heard that there was tin to be had in the wonderful country of Tarshish, at the other end of the Mediterranean, and the lure of that treasure was great enough for them to conquer their fears of the unknown.

A legend tells of the great god Melkart arriving one day at the end of the world—Gibraltar. At that time Gibraltar was joined to Africa, and so the Mediterranean was enclosed. Melkart cleft the land, forming the Straits, and set up a pillar on either side. Melkart is none other than the Greek Heracles and the Roman Hercules, and these were the famous Pillars of Hercules erected by the hero of antiquity when he fought Geryon, King of Tarshish. The Pillar on the European side was called Calpe, and the other Abyle. According to this

Iberian lion

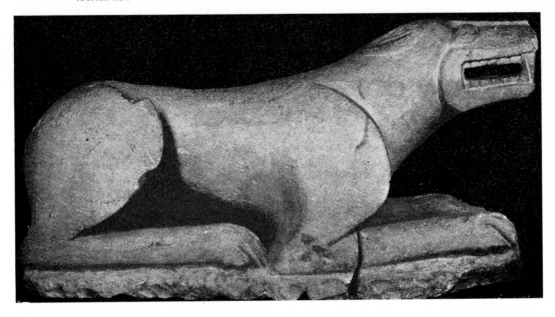

123

legend, of which there are many versions, the King of Tyre was ordered by the gods to found a colony near these Pillars. He sent three advance parties, last of which was welcomed by the god and the population, founded the town of Gadir, and soon made it a prosperous colony.

We can see in these legends the great historical feat of the Phoenicians—the discovery of the Atlantic Ocean. They did not, however, at once venture across this billowing sea, but

Iberian
glazed
pottery

proceeded cautiously by sending observers along the coast to study the navigational problems of the unknown waters.

As it happened, these merchant-venturers were not far from Tarshish. Following their usual custom, they first settled on a small island off the coast and there founded Gadir (called Gades by the Greeks, now known as Cadiz). The settlement soon became an important post for trade between the Phoenicians and Tarshish. The splendid products of Tyre were there bartered for copper, silver and gold, and the much-sought-after tin. Tarshish did not supply a great deal of tin, but from their new base the Phoenicians were able to reach more distant lands, the "tin islands," where it was found in abundance. Aristotle relates that a Phoenician ship was so laden with merchandise that an amount of silver was in danger of being left behind. But the crew solved the problem by exchanging the ship's copper anchors for silver ones. The natives probably did not know the relative

124

Coin from Tartessus. with Phoenician lettering

value of the two metals, and the Phoenicians were certainly not the people to enlighten them.

The date when Gadir was founded is usually put at 1100 B.C., in which case it would have been the oldest Tyrian colony. But this is only inspired guesswork, and the general belief is that Utica and other North African towns were founded before Gadir. The actual date is not very important. The main fact is that the Phoenicians established a line of fortified colonies to ensure free passage for their ships and, especially, to prevent rivals from following in their wake.

Gadir was an excellent trading post, situated as it was on a beautiful island just off the coast. It had a sheltered harbor, and could be easily defended against enemy attack. Other Phoenician colonies were established along the south coast of the Iberian peninsula—among them Malcha (Malaga), Abdera, and Sexti. It is interesting to note that the Phoenicians, who had little notion of agriculture, were never attracted by the fertile Andalusian plains. They had thoughts only of the sea, and all their efforts were concentrated on trade.

"This land of the Iberians has more and richer silver mines than any other country. But its inhabitants had no idea of the value of the metal until the Phoenicians appeared with their merchant ships and bought vast quantities of silver . . . [for which they gave a very small quantity of goods]. They carried this

Ancient Iberian writing tablet, with letters believed to be Tartessian

125

silver to Greece, Asia and other parts, amassing much wealth in the process. This kind of transaction went on for many years, enabling them to acquire considerable power and to establish many colonies in Sicily and the neighboring islands, in Africa, Sardinia and even in Spain." There is no reason to disbelieve these words by such an eminent historian as Diodorus of Sicily. The Phoenicians made great profits with little effort by trading with backward peoples who were unaware of the value of their metals. The idea of using silver as a means of payment had not then been conceived, so the natives willingly gave their metals in exchange for various manufactured articles.

Phoenician ship

The rapidly developing town of Gadir soon supplanted Tarshish. There is some vague evidence of a struggle between the two, which lasted some time. Then comes a complete blank, as the Tyrians left no records and nothing certain is known of Tarshish itself. There are several references in the Old Testament to the Tarshish voyages of the Phoenicians, notably during the time of King Hiram of Tyre. A few Greek and Roman writers also make some mention of Tarshish, but we do not even know just where the ancient city stood.

Archaeologists have labored to discover traces of Tarshish, but to no avail. The German archaeologist and historian, A. Schulten, who spent his life seeking the site, wrote with some bitterness that the small, insignificant town of Troy is famed to this day because of the work of a poet, whereas the greatest cultural center of ancient Europe has completely vanished from history, after being laid waste by the Carthaginians. Towns and civilizations, like literary works, are subject to fate. Luck, that frivolous goddess, may one day smile upon those who are still seeking Tarshish. According to one of the most popularly held theories, Tarshish was at the mouth of the river Beatis (or Tartessos), now known as the Guadalquivir. But the salt waters of the Atlantic seem to have combined with the fresh water of this great river to hide all trace of Tarshish from prying eyes. Many other possible sites of Tarshish have been named, and there will be no end to the argument until some archaeologist, luckier than the others, can find indisputable evidence of the site.

The simplest answer to the mystery, of course, is that Tarshish never existed, that it was merely a symbol. But the facts are not so simple. There are references in ancient writings to Tarshish as a real town. Hebrews, Greeks, Assyrians, Romans, all mention the city-state of Tarshish, blessed by the heavens and overflowing with wealth. The stories and legends in themselves suffice to

126

testify to its existence. And there are the many references in the Bible to Tarshish ships and voyages to Tarshish. When the prophet Jonah tried to flee from the Lord, where did he think of going? To Tarshish—the farthest known point in the West. He went down to Joppa and "found a ship going to Tarshish; so he paid the fare thereof, and went down into it, to go with them unto Tarshish from the presence of the Lord." (Jonah, 1:3.)

Strabo, the energetic Roman geographer, stated that the people of Tarshish were the most advanced of all the peoples of the Iberian peninsula, that they could read and write. They wrote down their history, composed poems, dealt in metals, and were bold seamen. According to Strabo, Tarshish was devastated by the Phoenicians (or Carthaginians) after a great naval battle in which all the Tarshish ships were sunk or burnt. This strange account has a similarity with the legend of the war between Melkart-Hercules and Geryon. In Strabo's story the king of Tarshish was called Tyron.

Troy had no existence before Schliemann discovered it. The site of Tarshish has not yet been revealed to archaeologists, but the city shines in all its glory in ancient writings.

Fragment of antique painted pottery, bearing recognizable Iberian lettering the meaning of which is indecipherable

127

Vase, from Liria in Spain,
in glazed pottery, showing
orchestra of musicians

When and by whom was this marvelous city founded? Schulten puzzled over this problem for twenty-seven years. His perseverance had its reward, but his conclusion—that the Etruscans founded Tarshish—was very surprising. The eminent historian arrived at it by etymological and philological deductions which take up many pages of his book on Tarshish. But his reasoning is based on such subtle and slender clues that no one is convinced. According to Schulten, Tarshish is the Greek form of the name Tartessos—that is to say, the town of the Tirses or Etruscans. And it was founded about 1200 B.C., simply because the people of Tarshish may well have been the "Peoples of the Sea" who had invaded Egypt at that period. Egyptian inscriptions certainly mention the Tirses, who after their defeat in Egypt made their way to the West and settled in Italy and Spain. Another twenty-seven years will probably be needed to unravel this tangle, but it would be worth the trouble.

Vase painting,
from Liria in Spain,
showing mounted soldiers

128

PLATE 8

Judean ship of the third century B.C.

Designed by M. Pliner and built by M. I. Krupnik from a mural engraving found .in the catacombs of Beit Shearim. Despite a certain imprecision, which is unsatisfactory for model-making, it has been possible to reconstruct here an adequate general idea of the Jewish ships of this period. They do not differ essentially in construction from those which had been sailing the Mediterranean as long ago as the eighteenth and nineteenth centuries B.C.· of the type known as "round ships" as opposed to the long ships that relied primarily upon the oar and were used for war rather than for commerce. This round ship has a sail of trapezoid shape, which is a stage intermediate between the rectangular square sail of antiquity and the triangular lateen sail still used in the Mediterranean today. This ship had no oars at all, and the double steering oars are of the pattern seen in Roman ships. The approximate length would be 15 or 16 meters with a displacement of 70 to 90 metric tons.

PLATE 8

Judean ship of the third century B.C.

Putting aside etymology, there exist plenty of historical sources to show that in the second millennium there was a flourishing trade in metals in the Iberian peninsula. Even today, traces of mine workings and metal industries can be seen. They indicate that four to five thousand years ago the West supplied the raw materials, while the East—having the knowledge and skill—concentrated on manufactures. It may be that Tarshish was not only the meeting place for traders between the East and West, but also a center for peoples along the Atlantic coast. Evidence is lacking for any assertion on this point, but it does seem within the bounds of possibility. The great industrial prosperity of the period 2000–1500 B.C. is difficult to account for unless there was an adequate supply of raw materials and considerable enterprise by merchant-venturers.

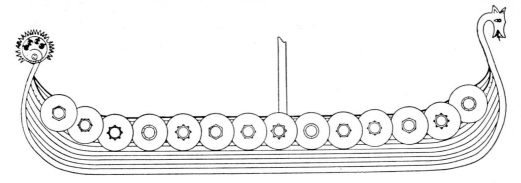

Schematic drawing of Viking
ship. The resemblance of
its hull line to that of
certain Phoenician types is
probably not accidental

ACROSS THE WILD OCEAN

To the ancients, the Atlantic was the turbulent domain of
Poseidon, into whose affairs the civilized, obliging gods of
Olympus should not intrude. Death reigned over that limitless
stretch of wild waters, death in a thousand different guises—
hunger and thirst, icy cold, sea monsters and sirens, choking
plants that held ships in their grip for months ... there was
no end to the tales. What fears must have been in the minds
of the first Tyrians to sail out of the known world of the
Mediterranean.

They soon realized that all the terrible stories about the
Atlantic were mere myths and fables born of man's fears and
imagination. Nevertheless, they continued to spread them, and
even invented new ones—to deter trade rivals. But as adventurers
are not always put off by frightening tales, the Phoenicians
relied more on their chain of fortified colonies and settlements.
The two on either side of the Straits of Gibraltar—Gadir and
Tingis (Tangier)—completed their strategic positions from one
end of the Mediterranean to the other: Tyre, Cyprus, Cythera,
Leptis Magna, Utica, Malta, Sicily, Sardinia, and the Balearics.

Terrifying stories about the Atlantic—the "Wild West"—
continued to circulate among Mediterranean seamen for
hundreds of years after their ships had begun to sail the ocean
more or less regularly. This is understandable, for to the ancients
the Atlantic was a very different proposition from the
Mediterranean.

131

The Mediterranean gives confidence, it entices far more than it deters. The profusion of islands almost reduces navigation to a simple ferry service. Harborage is plentiful, under the lee of numerous headlands and islands that also serve admirably as direction posts. Land and sea breezes blow with regularity, and the general absence of tideways, shoals and strong currents greatly facilitates inshore navigation. The Mediterranean winds shift according to simple and regular laws, and for much of the year one cloudless, clear day is followed by another. The night sky is correspondingly clear. How different, then, was the

Terra-cotta siren from Athens

unpredictable ocean beyond the straits. No island haven within sight there, when a gale suddenly springs up; only great waves and black clouds piling up, an immensity of sea and a howling wind. The Atlantic has its smooth, smiling moments, but they do not last for long. Furthermore, it has not the calm, serene and graceful smile of the Mediterranean, but rather the hearty laugh of a rough giant sure of his strength. To the ancient Mediterranean seafarer the Atlantic was indeed a cruel sea, intractable and fickle, like life itself, offering only toil and trouble without any certainty of reward—a sorry prospect for the faint-hearted. But for the bold who defied the ocean, there was the satisfaction that comes from striving and the joy of victory.

When seas are rough the modern ship has little to fear, and

132

many liners are equipped with stabilizers. But what of the ancients in their wooden sailing boats, tossed like cockleshells on the cresting waves? How were they to appease the gods who, for reasons beyond mortal understanding, had suddenly begun to blow and to scream with rage? Fortunately the gods had their weaknesses, too. The Phoenicians and Greeks alike were quite convinced that the waves and the winds, being gods or sons of gods, would calm down at the sight of a pretty, naked young woman. This was the reason that the ancients often had a young woman or two on board—possibly they sometimes shared them with the gods. The gods, however, had much to do, and sometimes failed to notice them.

We should not scoff at such absurd beliefs, for to some extent they helped the Phoenicians, in pursuit of riches, to overcome their fears and defy the elements.

In their days, time was of little account. A voyage that took the Phoenician away from home for two or three years was a normal occurrence. He had unlimited patience, and the idea that time is money never entered his head. A long voyage generally brought him much profit, but he did not count the time spent over it. He could endure great suffering and was indifferent to heat and cold, rain and hail, and he sailed equably to the chilly north or down the coast of tropical Africa. But when he reached port he believed in enjoying himself, in making up for his long abstinence. The peoples with whom he came into contact were severely critical of his behavior, though today we find it only natural for sailors to seek easy pleasures at the end of a long voyage.

Gadir was the first Phoenician colony in Spain and the springboard for later ventures. The city eventually imposed its domination over Tarshish, not only because of the latter's great wealth but also because its seamen were capable of reaching the "tin islands" by their own means. The Phoenicians, and the Carthaginians after them, guarded the secrets of their markets and seaways most jealously, and allowed no foreign ship to pass between the Pillars of Hercules. The Phoenicians made huge profits from their trade with the tin islands, so it was well worth their while to protect their interests. Capitalists in antiquity did not act very differently from those of today.

Some historians have advanced the theory that the Phoenicians founded a kingdom in southern England, and that they built a settlement on the site of London long before the Romans. This theory is based on the fact that many Phoenician coins and objects have been discovered in the south of England. But they prove no more than that trade relations between the inhabitants of England and the Phoenicians were well established. The latter therefore had no need to occupy the area, especially as they controlled the sea route.

There was also an overland route from the Mediterranean to the tin islands, and the Phoenicians could do nothing to prevent the flow of trade along it. In any case, the traders in the north were as secretive about their overland route as the Phoenicians were about their sea routes.

Whether the Phoenicians ever sailed beyond England and crossed the North Sea to the Scandinavian countries is a matter for conjecture. During the Bronze Age there were apparently "long ships" in use in Swedish waters that had great similarity to Phoenician ships. This hardly constitutes a proof of the Phoenicians having reached Sweden. Nevertheless, Viking ships had similar lines to "Tarshish ships," and the possibility of Mediterranean sailors having reached Scandinavian waters in quite early times cannot be entirely ruled out.

On the other hand, no doubt exists as to their discovery of the Canaries. From Gadir and Tingis, the Phoenicians sailed down the west coast of Africa in search of something more important to them than tin or silver or even gold—the means of making purple dye. The necessary shellfish had practically disappeared from eastern Mediterranean waters, and the purple-dye industry was a greater source of wealth even than the Tarshish trade. The Phoenicians who sailed south diligently explored the shores and islands in search of a supply of the precious shellfish. Continuing on, they discovered Madeira and the Canaries, where they found what they were seeking. It was not a shellfish, though, but a tree, the *dracoena draco*. It exuded a deep red resin that was found to be suitable for making purple dye. Luck was on the side of the Phoenicians, for they also came across an aromatic plant, the *roccela tinctoria*, that could be used for making the dye.

The excitement when news of these discoveries reached Tyre can be imagined, for the purple-dye industry was given a new lease on life. Moreover, those great rivals of the Phoenicians, the Greeks, had been forestalled. They, too, were trying to make purple dye and were faced with the same crucial problem, a great shortage of raw material. They spied on the Phoenicians, tried to follow their ships, made war in order to take over their colonies, knowing quite well that wherever the Phoenicians pitched their tents there was usually abundant wealth to be gained. It is difficult for us today to realize the immense value

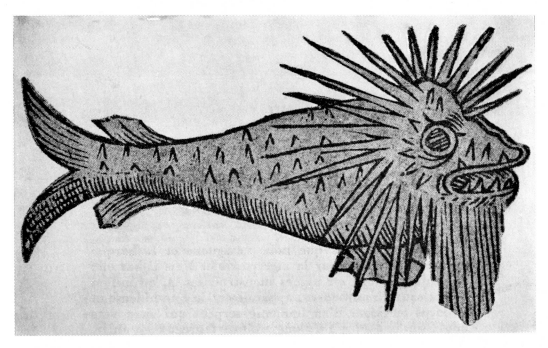

**Sea monster from
illuminated manuscript of
the voyage of St. Brendan**

and prestige the ancients attached to purple cloth. The Greeks
and others were astounded when the Tyrians began producing
new supplies of it.

The Phoenicians tried to keep their new discoveries a close
secret, but even in those times sailors liked to boast of their
experiences, which were embellished in the telling by a lively
imagination. After a few drinks in some Mediterranean port
with a pretty young woman for company, the Phoenician sailors
told stories that roused other people's imagination, and reached
a wider public in the form of myths and legends. Somewhere
out at sea, beyond the known world, were islands with a warm
and gentle climate; the soil was most fertile, and the ground
contained great riches. To the Greeks, these islands could be
none other than the "Islands of the Blessed," producing a wealth
greater even than that of Tarshish.

The purple dye obtained from plants on these islands gave
fresh life to the industry, which spread to Carthage, since it was
much nearer than Tyre to the source of supplies. The resin

135

provided a much greater quantity of purple dye than had ever been obtained from shellfish, and Carthage developed the industry to a larger extent than Tyre had ever done.

After the fall of Carthage all knowledge of these blessed islands was lost, and they were not discovered again till the Middle Ages, by Henry the Navigator. This Portuguese prince devoted all his wealth and energy to seeking out new lands, and was in no way deterred by the horrible tales about the Atlantic which were still current. When the Portuguese explorers discovered Madeira and the Azores they, in their turn, spread terrifying stories about these regions.

The Islands of the Blessed may have been the Hesperides to which Hercules was sent to bring back the golden apples. But modern geographers have had a grand time trying to identify all the place names in Homer and in Greek legends generally. In any case, the Greeks transported the "Garden of the Hesperides" (where a dragon guarded the golden apples) to the far west—a sufficient reason for the cruel Mycenaean king to send Hercules there. The real meanings behind all these legends and myths will probably never be known, but there will always be scholars trying to find them.

Many legends indicate that America had been discovered long before the time of Columbus. The Vikings certainly seem to have made the crossing, and there are even tales of the Irish and the Basques preceding the Vikings in finding a route to America. However, there is no proof behind these tales, and men are always sceptical of anything not "on paper."

Some eccentric philologists have tried to establish that the Phoenicians reached America. They base their argument on the fact that the languages of certain South American Indian tribes have a distinct root resemblance to Hebrew or the language of the Canaanites. One of these specialists even reached the conclusion that the Mayas of Mexico had spoken pure Greek. Such ridiculous assertions are in the same category as the claim that the Gaelic people are the descendants of the ten lost tribes of Israel, chiefly of the Dan and Zabulon tribes, who are supposed to have settled in Ireland and Scotland. They apparently founded the kingdom of Dania too—modern Denmark—because Dania means in Hebrew "the country of the children of Dan." There is indeed no limit to the ardor of some "specialists" when determined to prove a pet theory.

Yet there must have been some fact or news item which set these philologists to work on the theory that the Phoenicians landed on the American continent. It may be found in the

136

**Phoenician ornament
of legendary beasts**

work of a Brazilian scholar who, in 1899, communicated the text of an inscription he had discovered high on a rock not far from Rio de Janeiro. It told of the sufferings endured by Canaanites after landing on that coast, of their torments from heat and thirst. Their one consolation had been in Baal. Scholars argued interminably over the inscription, though they generally agreed that the writing was Phoenician of a late period, in use at the time of the fall of Carthage. The assumption was not easily dismissed, for the Carthaginians were experienced seamen and some might have fled in their ships before the arrival of the Romans. However, when scholars finally concluded that the inscription was a fake, they were unanimous in their decision. But in that case one is bound to wonder why a person or persons should scale a rock to carve in Phoenician writing praises to Baal and reports of human sufferings. Admittedly, there has always been a trade in fake scrolls, tablets and parchments, but buyers could be found for them, whereas an ancient inscription on a high rock . . .

An even stranger story came to light in more recent years. A Brazilian rubber planter, Don Bernardo da Silva Ramos, discovered an inscription on a rock three thousand feet up in the mountains behind Rio de Janeiro, and he made out the words: "Tyre, the Canaanite Baalezer, eldest of Etbaal."

Itobaal, or Etbaal, is known to have been a high priest of Baal and King of Tyre in 887–856 B.C. If the inscription were authentic, it must have been carved in the latter half of the ninth century B.C. Brazilian scholars did not proclaim this one a fake; they merely affirmed—according to the writer Paul Herrmann, who had asked the Brazilian Ministry of Education—that it was not writing at all, but marks made by rain and rivulets and the elements in general, which chanced to resemble an

137

ancient form of writing. So nature had played a trick on man —and on a high, smooth rock face near a hill resort called Pedro da Gavia!

Don Bernardo refused to accept this explanation. He was wealthy and had a stubborn character. He sold his rubber plantations and thenceforth devoted all his time and energy to his various hobbies, which included numismatics. For many years he searched the Amazon jungles for evidence of contact between the American continent and the Mediterranean world of antiquity. His penetrating eye discovered many rocks and boulders bearing markings that resembled Phoenician writing and ancient Greek. In the course of twenty years he photographed and classified more than three thousand such inscriptions. When one thinks of the climate and conditions in the Amazon region, one is forced to admire Don Bernardo's stamina and faith in his task.

The physical sufferings he must have endured were followed by moral sufferings when he published his account and translations of the inscriptions in 1939. Brazilian scholars gave no credence to his work, and he became an object of their mockery. This eccentric had spent his money and talents on researches which had no meaning. But the inscriptions and markings on the rocks and boulders undoubtedly exist; and the world of scholars has made mistakes more than once. Perhaps someday Don Bernardo will be proved right after all. At least his work may help to solve an exciting mystery.

There are many indications of contacts between Europe and America in very early times—indications that the persisting currents and breezes which carried Columbus across the Atlantic could have driven previous travelers. Legends of the Incas and the Aztecs contain allusions to white men who reached their shores from some unknown land. And there are references in Greek and Roman writers to transatlantic voyages. Pomponius Mela, a contemporary of Julius Caesar, wrote of Metellus Celer, who was proconsul of Gaul in 59 B.C., receiving from the king of a Celtic tribe a present of some "Indians" said to have been cast up on the coast of Gaul. Could these unfortunates have been Indians of the red variety? They had certainly not come from Asia, but it is conceivable that their boat could have been blown across the Atlantic without being swamped. Whether there was any truth in the anecdote is impossible to say, but in any case it indicates that something was known of the people living on the other side of the Atlantic.

A yet stranger tale was told to Pausanias (c. A.D. 170), that a ship belonging to a certain Euphemus of Caria was blown through the Straits of Gibraltar and across the ocean to an island inhabited by redskins with horses' tails who frightened the newcomers away by their menacing attitude. Plato wrote of another continent's existing across the Atlantic, and similar mention can be found in Seneca, Eratosthenes, Cornelius Nepos, and many other ancient writers. But there exists no evidence that the ancients actually discovered America. It is possible, however, that ships were blown across the ocean and reached strange shores, against the desires of the crews. Modern expeditions have demonstrated the possibility of using the ocean currents to cross from one continent to another in ancient craft.

The Phoenicians had discovered the Canaries and Madeira, and the Carthaginians may have reached the Azores. From these islands, or from farther down the west coast of Africa, vessels could well have been carried by winds and currents to the coast of Brazil. The discoveries made by Don Bernardo da Silva should not, therefore, be so lightly dismissed. Indeed, his memory may one day receive due honor, for the controversy over his inscriptions still continues, and many people strongly believe there was contact between Europe and America long before the time of Columbus.

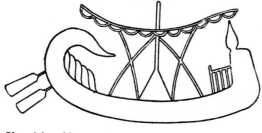

Phoenician ship

Chapter 16

SOLOMON AND HIRAM:

A ROYAL ASSOCIATION

Very early in their history the Phoenicians had opened up an overland route to India for their merchant caravans. In the minds of Western peoples, then as now, the Orient stood for exotic romance and colorful legend. The Phoenicians, whose ships eventually sailed the Indian Ocean, were the go-betweens of these two parts of the world, carrying not only merchandise from one to the other but opening up new horizons of culture.

The amount of goods that could be carried overland was much less than could be carried by sea. Maritime transport has always been, and still is, the cheapest of all, so the Phoenicians became very active in seeking access to the Red Sea, to provide passage into the Indian Ocean for their ships. Their relations with the Egyptians dated back to very early times, and Phoenician traders had even been given permission to establish a colony in the Delta. And from the Delta there was an outlet to the Red Sea by way of the "Suez Canal."

Tyre was in the ascendant, but Egyptian power was beginning to wane. Her pharaohs feared that the canal might be used by invaders, and so had ceased to maintain it. Drifting sand blocked it in places, and it was of no help to the Phoenicians.

Another solution was sought. The Kingdom of Judah had an outlet to the Red Sea, and the Hebrews and the Phoenician-Canaanites had always lived on the best of terms. Any difficulties

141

that had arisen between these two neighboring countries had always been smoothed away by diplomatic means. They were bound by common interests and to some extent by kinship and language. Although racial affinity, of course, has never been a guarantee of peace between nations.

Truth is not well served by those historians who maintain that the Phoenicians were Hebrews. The King of Tyre addressed the King of Israel as "my brother," their subjects were on amicable terms, and marriages were often contracted between the border peoples. But it does not follow that the Tyrians were of the Hebrew race.

The King of Tyre at the beginning of the tenth century B.C. was an enlightened and farsighted monarch named Hiram, son of Abi-Baal. He extended the boundaries of his city and made it a better and finer place to live. He encouraged industry and the arts, and consolidated trade relations with Egypt, thus making sure of the friendship of the pharaohs. At that period the Assyrians were sapping their strength in continual fighting against the Babylonians, their neighbors and rivals, so they presented no threat to Tyre.

Israel, extending south from Tyre, had previously been a weak kingdom threatened by enemies on all sides and split by internal dissension. Then King David succeeded in defeating the bordering states and in making Israel a united and powerful kingdom. David was a warrior king who in those troubled times was able to give a sense of unity and national pride to his people. But the road to peace is fraught with hidden dangers, and King David experienced the painful road by which men reach the heights. He paid for his success both as a politician and as a man, but he was known for his intensely human qualities. King Hiram shrewdly judged David's genius and liked his impulsive character. Foreseeing the greatness of Israel, he made friendly overtures to David, sending gifts and offering to help with the building of the Temple in Jerusalem. David was unable to realize this ambition, which was left to his son Solomon to complete.

We read in the First Book of Kings (4:25) that Solomon had peace in his reign. "And Judah and Israel dwelt safely, every man under his vine and under his fig tree, from Dan even to Beer-sheba, all the days of Solomon." Solomon had not inherited his father's passionate temperament; his qualities were his wisdom—renowned to this day—his calm, thoughtful nature and his powers of reasoning. Such was the outward calm and the self-control of this monarch that no record exists of his personal life as a man. He was the perfect example of the enlightened oriental ruler, serene and dignified, wise and alert in his experience. But Solomon also possessed great organizing ability, and behind that serene brow ideas abounded that urged him on to intense activity throughout his reign. He divided his kingdom into twelve provinces or regions and set up a sound administration in each. He created new towns and rebuilt those that had been devastated by war. He built forts, supply depots and fortified outposts (the "cities of store" of the Bible), and made roads as much to attract foreign merchant caravans into the country as for the benefit of his own people's travels. He began to exploit the natural resources of the Negev and other regions. There were many quarries in Israel, and in Solomon's time the stonecutting industry was greatly developed. The building of the Temple, which took thirteen years, called for enormous quantities of stone. Much stone was also used in the construction of garrison towns, and building in general made great progress. Everything known about Solomon indicates that he was a wise ruler, and that he greatly increased the heritage received from his father.

These building and development schemes called for huge sums of money, and in addition there was the cost of administration and the army. The natural resources of the country were not sufficient to meet these demands, and Solomon began to think of the great profits to be made from international trade. There was an excellent example in the neighboring kingdom of Tyre. Israel was at the center of trade routes between Tyre

The temple of Solomon

and Mesopotamia, Tyre and Arabia, and Egypt and Babylonia. The newly made roads and the peaceful conditions soon attracted merchant caravans to Israel. But Solomon in his wisdom had far greater ambitions for the economic development of his country. He wanted to export its products and by the cheapest means of transport—in other words, by ship. For that he needed good harbors and, of course, a fleet of merchant ships.

Solomon was the first and probably the only King of Israel who really understood the importance of the sea. The country's prosperity and to a certain extent its security depended upon its sea power and its relations with the maritime states.

However, most of the Mediterranean coast was held by the Philistines, and, although King David had subdued them, Solomon would very likely have had to employ force to make use of their harbors for his own purposes. The coast to the north (lands of the tribes of Asher and Naphtali) gave Solomon access to the Mediterranean, but the harbors there were poor. The really good harbors were those of the Tyrians. Solomon was well aware that Israel was in no position to wage war on Tyre. In fact, in order to build a fleet and to sail the seas freely, an amicable understanding with Tyre had to be reached. Tyre possessed great experience of the sea and was rich in maritime traditions. Ambitious though he was, Solomon had a realistic outlook. To compete against the interests of Tyre would in no way advance his prospects of entering the sea-carrying trade. What, then, was the solution? Israel had an outlet to the Red Sea, across the Negev. This southern region was almost a desert, a wilderness, but Solomon saw it to be the key to his problem— a proposition of great interest to Tyre on which he could base his negotiations.

It was one of those rare instances in history of two neighboring countries seeking economic expansion and each finding an aid in the other.

King Hiram's policy, too, was based on peace and on the maintenance of friendly relations with Israel, which was a useful market for the timber and manufactured goods of the Phoenicians. Moreover, the Hebrews were then considered doughty warriors who had often had good fortune on their side. Such neighbors were entitled to every consideration.

In a relatively short time Solomon transformed Israel from an essentially agricultural country into a prosperous industrial one, chiefly by seeking and bringing in technicians and specialists from outside. There were, for instance, deposits of copper in the Negev, but the Hebrews had little knowledge of how to exploit

144

PLATE 9

Phoenician or Assyrian bireme
of about the eighth century B.C.

This ship was reconstructed by M. Pliner and M. I. Krupnik from a bas-relief from the place at Nineveh, which is now in the British Museum, made to the order of King Sennacherib.

It is a typical warship in length and narrowness of beam, armed with a ram at the forefoot of the prow, which was a weapon much feared at this period when there were hardly any missile weapons capable of sinking a ship. There is an upper foredeck for the use exclusively of the soldiers, whose shields are seen hung along the bulwarks above a rowing deck on which the galley slaves sit. This ship had two banks each with 7 to 12 oars on either side, as well as a square sail on a single mast. This arrangement of oars in two banks, followed later by the triremes, or ships with three banks of oars, first came into being in the eighth century and became standard equipment for the navies of antiquity, though it is still imperfectly understood by archaeologists exactly how these oars and their rowers were arranged. This type of warship, with its long, narrow, streamlined hull, is found frequently in the design of Phoenician coins.

PLATE 9

Phoenician or Assyrian bireme
of about the eighth century B.C.

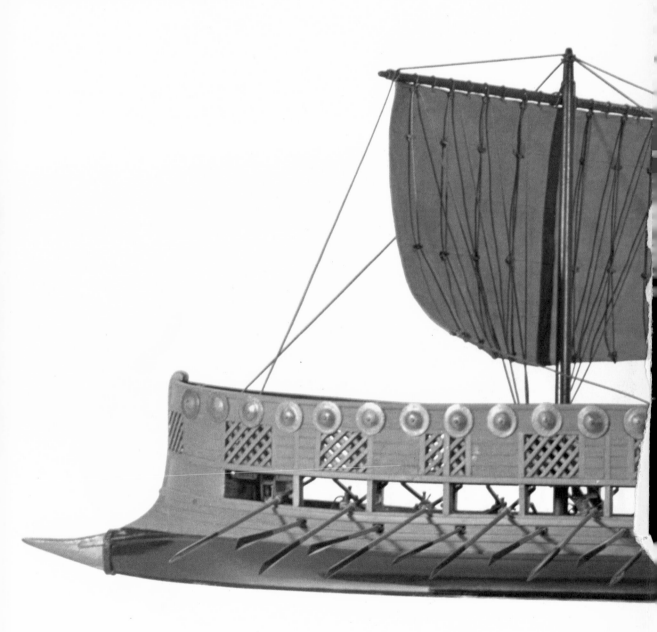

them. The metalworker from Tyre, Hiram, who was mentioned in an earlier chapter, undoubtedly had other Tyrian specialists working with him on Solomon's Temple. Some of them may well have started the foundries in the Negev, which were perhaps the largest that have ever existed. The processes in use in these foundries were later forgotten and lost to the world until they were rediscovered by Bessemer. For many centuries, the tales in the Bible of Solomon's great treasures and wisdom were thought by many readers to be no more than oriental fables. It was only in quite recent years that an eminent archaeologist provided proof that King Solomon's copper mines had really existed. The site of the foundries was known to have been near the coastal town of Ezion-Geber, built by Solomon as part of his development plans. All trace of it had disappeared, and archaeologists searched for it unsuccessfully for many years, until an American, Nelson Glueck, chanced upon it. He was directing excavations at an isolated spot called Tel El Halaifa, and almost from the start the remains of a large town began to come to light. It was a town which had obviously been planned and built as a whole, and was undoubtedly the Ezion-Geber of the Bible. When the children of Israel had passed into Egypt, they went through the land of Edom and by the town of Ezion-Geber (Deuteronomy 2:8). But the town unearthed by Nelson Glueck had not been built on the site of an older town; it was obviously part of Solomon's national planning scheme, a "new town." It had been a large one for the times, covering nearly three square miles. The walls had been twenty-five feet high and twelve feet thick in places, proof of its great importance. The main gate faced the sea. If a sea-borne invader had succeeded in storming into the town, he would have found himself faced by a second fortified gate and in an open square surrounded by high walls—trapped, in fact, and an easy mark for the arrows of the defenders. Some of the fortified towns built by Solomon were given a third inner gate within a walled square.

The published theories of Nelson Glueck, based upon his archaeological findings, were later refuted in an article written by a young Israeli scholar, Benno Rothenberg, who claimed that King Solomon's copper mines had been some fifty miles north of the place where Glueck had sited them. However, Rothenberg has not yet published an account of his own excavations, and the argument is unresolved for the moment.

In any case, discoveries already made are sufficient to demonstrate that metal industries were extensive in the Negev, and that Ezion-Geber was the port from which the output was

145

shipped. This new port could not fail to interest the Phoenicians. King Hiram had ships and shipbuilding yards and timber, but Solomon had the port which provided an outlet to the Red Sea and the Indian Ocean, offering an expansion of trade with Africa, Arabia, and India. The two monarchs therefore had common interests, and this is probably an explanation of the friendly relations which existed between them for so long. It also provides an explanation of an odd passage in the Old Testament: "And Hiram sent to the King [Solomon] six score talents of gold. And this is the reason for the levy which King Solomon raised; for to build the house of the Lord, and his own house, and Millo, and the wall of Jerusalem, and Hazor, and Megiddo, and Gezer." (I Kings 9:14, 15.)

Why should Hiram have had to pay such a great sum to Solomon? Tyre had not been conquered by Solomon's army; in fact there was never war between the two kingdoms. The answer, it can now be seen, is that the gold and technical assistance were given by Tyre in exchange for transit rights and use of the port on the shores of the Red Sea. Port dues already existed in Solomon's time, and they were very heavy.

It is unlikely that the visit of the Queen of Sheba to Jerusalem was undertaken merely through courtesy or out of curiosity. King Solomon's fame had spread far and wide, but one can hardly believe that the Queen of Sheba made a long and exhausting journey just to satisfy herself that he was really the wisest of men. Wisdom has never been one of the chief attractions that women find in men. And not even the most curious of women would be prepared to pay such a price for an interview with Solomon. "And she gave the king an hundred and twenty talents of gold, and of spices very great store, and precious stones; there came no more such abundance of spices as these which the Queen of Sheba gave to King Solomon." (I Kings 10:10.)

Any journey in those days was slow and difficult, even for a monarch. The Queen of Sheba must have had a definite aim in mind, either to "buy" herself a famous husband or to obtain trade concessions which would add even more to her great wealth. Perhaps both!

Marriage, however, was almost certainly not the object of her visit. She must have heard of the number of Solomon's wives; and an independent, rich monarch such as she was hardly likely to share a husband. Her mission would seem to have been connected with the marketing of the spices of southern Arabia. The Queen wanted to negotiate the taxes that Solomon wished to

146

impose on goods in transit. Women have always had a keen commercial sense. If they bring grace and beauty to the negotiations, it makes them all the more pleasant. In any case, those between Solomon and the Queen of Sheba remained a secret. No palace scribes were present at the meetings to make notes, which is a pity.

Tyrean necklace in gold and paste

Chapter 17

THE GOLD OF OPHIR

Few passages in the Bible can have given rise to so much conjecture or caused so much argument as those relating to the association of Solomon and Hiram in fitting out a fleet to bring back gold from Ophir. In the First Book of Kings we read: "And King Solomon made a navy of ships in Ezion-Geber, which is beside Eloth, on the shore of the Red Sea, in the land of Edom. And Hiram sent in the navy his servants, shipmen that had knowledge of the sea, with the servants of Solomon. And they came to Ophir, and fetched from thence gold, four hundred and twenty talents, and brought it to King Solomon." (9:26-28.)

A slightly different version is given in the Second Book of Chronicles: "Then went Solomon to Ezion-Geber, and to Eloth, at the sea side in the land of Edom. And Hiram sent him by the hands of his servants ships, and servants that had knowledge of the sea; and they went with the servants of Solomon to Ophir, and took thence four hundred and fifty talents of gold, and brought them to King Solomon." (8:17, 18.)

The two versions are agreed that Hiram sent seamen and shipbuilders to Ezion-Geber to build a fleet, and that the ships sailed to Ophir and returned. And corroboration is provided by the Phoenician priest and historian, Sanchoniaton, as quoted by Philo of Byblos, though in view of the fact that none of the writings of Sanchoniaton has survived, it is impossible to say whether he really existed or was just a fictional character created by Philo to give authority to his own chronicles. Be that as it may, Philo reported that, according to Sanchoniaton, Hiram, King of Tyre, sent eight thousand camels (*sic*) laden with timber to Ezion-Geber, for the building of ten ships.

149

Ophir is another legendary land which scholars and travelers have been trying to identify for centuries. Treasure-seekers have endeavored to discover this fabulous place which supplied Solomon with such huge quantities of gold. His Temple had gold everywhere: "And the oracle in the forepart was twenty cubits in length, and twenty cubits in breadth, and twenty cubits in the height thereof; and he overlaid it with pure gold; and so covered the altar which was of cedar. So Solomon overlaid the house within with pure gold; and he made a partition by the chains of gold before the oracle; and he overlaid it with gold. And the whole house he overlaid with gold." (I Kings 6:20–22.)

Solomon's great throne was overlaid with pure gold, as were the six steps to the throne, and all his drinking vessels were of gold. In a single year his Treasury received one hundred and seventy talents of gold, which did not include "that which chapmen and merchants brought. And all the kings of Arabia and governors of the country brought gold and silver to Solomon." (II Chronicles 9:14.) There was so much gold in the country that silver lost its value—"it was not any thing accounted of in the days of Solomon." In the King's treasure house, called "the house of the forest of Lebanon," there were placed "two hundred targets of beaten gold; six hundred shekels of gold went to one target. And he made three hundred shields of beaten gold; three pounds of gold went to one shield." (I Kings 10:16, 17.)

So much gold! It has been calculated that in one year Solomon accumulated more than fourteen tons of gold—enough to make seven hundred bars of it today! And that is not counting the gold brought in Tarshish ships. It is not surprising that so many people have dreamed of finding King Solomon's mines, and that for them—without success. Was there, then, ever such a place great sufferings have been endured and lives lost in searching as Ophir?

Several passages in the Old Testament speak quite definitely of the building of Solomon's ships by technicians sent from Tyre. "Tarshish ships" was the name the ancients generally gave to those of the Phoenicians. The existence of a port and industrial center on the shore of the Red Sea has been confirmed by recent excavations, which have also provided evidence in support of the biblical accounts of Solomon's building developments and his great riches. The only debatable point, the one difficult to accept, is this joint enterprise of Hiram and Solomon, the association of Phoenicians and Hebrews in a sea expedition. The trading methods of the Phoenicians were very different from those of their neighbors. They kept a close guard on their secrets, and were not above using force to prevent foreigners from intruding into their trading areas.

Was the outlet to the Red Sea the only reason for the Phoenicians entering into association with the Hebrews? Solomon would appear to have had everything to gain from it. He had neither the technicians to build the ships, the timber, nor the crews experienced in deep-sea navigation. He supplied neither money, technical ability, nor manpower for the enterprise. What, then, was the attraction for such wily and experienced men of business as the Phoenicians? They were putting a very great deal into it. Even the cutting down and sending of the timber to Ezion-Geber was a considerable undertaking.

In a recent book Paul Herrmann, a German historian, put forward the view that Solomon had something far more important than a Red Sea port to offer Hiram—he knew all about the land of Ophir and where it was to be found!

According to legends that grew up around his memory, Solomon had been told about Ophir by birds twittering in his ear. He was the friend of birds and understood their language. But this delightful explanation will not satisfy everyone, and a more likely solution is that he acquired the knowledge along with a wife.

Ophir might have been none other than the Land of Punt, the "God's land" and source of incense and gold of the Egyptians. The pharaohs knew where it was situated. In the course of centuries they had sent many expeditions there. Solomon, according to the Bible, married the daughter of a pharaoh. It is possible that part of her dowry was information—even maps— giving the position of the Land of Punt. Or perhaps the pharaoh revealed the secret to his new son-in-law in exchange for a percentage of the profits from future expeditions to Punt.

At that period, in the time of the twenty-first dynasty, Egypt was in decline and no longer able to fetch treasures from Punt. She lacked the impulse and the ships. The reigning pharaoh, however, was not Shishak (or Shishonek), as Paul Herrmann states; that pharaoh was the founder of the twenty-second dynasty and reigned from 945 to 925 B.C., which were the final years of Solomon's reign (973 to 939, or to 933 according to some authorities). And Solomon married a pharaoh's daughter soon after coming to the throne. Moreover, Shishak is known to have given refuge to Jeroboam and his followers, who were mortal enemies of Solomon, and Solomon's father-in-law was hardly likely to have harbored his enemies. During Solomon's reign the political and economic relations between Israel and Egypt were excellent. Israel bought chariots from Egypt and sold herds of horses procured in Asia Minor. Solomon turned away from Assyria and based his policy on an alliance with Egypt. It would therefore seem that his father-in-law was Siamon, the penultimate pharaoh of the twenty-first dynasty, who reigned from 976 to 958 B.C.

In any case, Paul Herrmann's theory that Ophir and Punt were one and the same would seem plausible. In the Second Book of Chronicles (9:21) there is a description of the cargoes brought back from Ophir: "Gold, and silver, ivory, and apes, and peacocks." These, with the addition of aromatic plants, were the chief cargoes brought back from Punt by the ships of Queen Hatshepsut, as she recorded on the walls of her temple at Deir el-Bahri.

If Ophir and Punt were indeed the same place, then it was probably in the gold-mining region of Rhodesia known today as Mashona. This is where the ruins of the great stronghold of Zimbabwe, first discovered a hundred years ago, still stand. The circumference of its walls was more than two miles, and they were thirty feet high in places and nearly ten feet thick. Parts of the stronghold are honeycombed with passages, and it was plainly designed against attack. The strange conical towers are similar to some found in Peru, Sardinia, and Mesopotamia. Experts have thought they show Etruscan influence. There is no doubt that the Etruscans reached Sardinia, but it is hardly likely that they sailed as far as Peru. A more probable explanation is that this type of tower was developed in different parts of the world at about the same time. Among the interesting finds at Zimbabwe were several statuettes of Astarte and some small idols with the head of an osprey, which are said to show Egyptian and Phoenician influences.

Ever since its discovery experts have been arguing about Zimbabwe. Why was this great fort built there in the middle of Africa—the only one of its kind for thousands of miles? Who built it? One theory is that it served as a collecting center for gold and merchandise to be taken to Sofala, the port on the East African coast in ancient times. The fort would have served as a warehouse and a shelter for the settlement in the event of an attack. But few experts believe that the settlement could have been Egyptian or Phoenician. It was too far away from the home bases, and a return voyage would have taken three years—if nothing untoward occurred on the way. Another

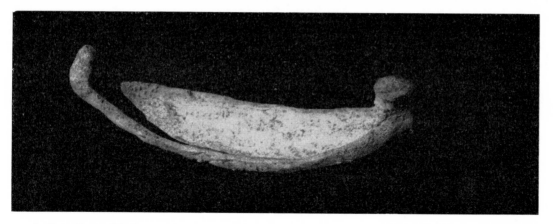

**Antique clay model of
Phoenician ship**

opinion is that the fort was constructed by Bantus, the tribe which settled in the region in the tenth century A.D. Again, a German geologist, Dr. Carl Mauch, who explored the ruins in 1871 and wrote an account of his find, thought the buildings were copies of King Solomon's Temple; for one thing, a feature of one part is walls within walls. However, a few years ago the Carbon-14 dating process was applied to a piece of timber from the fort, and its age was determined as dating back to the sixth century A.D. At that time there were no Bantus in the area, and the days of the Egyptians and the Phoenicians were long past. The possibility remains, of course, that Zimbabwe was originally an Egyptian settlement, was then taken over by Phoenicians and later abandoned by them, and was occupied hundreds of years later by nomad African tribes who repaired some of the ruins with timber.

The only fact upon which everyone agrees is that the tribes who inhabited the area around Zimbabwe when it was discovered in the last century had nothing to do with its construction. They lived in primitive huts, and looked upon the ruins as sacred. The Rhodesian authorities finally took over Zimbabwe, which is now protected by law. But it remains a riddle . . .

Paul Herrmann's theory, nevertheless, obtains greater plausibility. If the Ophir of the Old Testament and the Punt of the Egyptian inscriptions were indeed one and the same, then the business association of Hiram and Solomon is more easily explained.

In any case, Hiram would seem to have drawn far more benefit from it than Solomon. After the first expedition, which was almost certainly a combined undertaking, the Phoenicians

153

would have known as much about Ophir—wherever it was—as their associates. They had the ships and the seamen, and Solomon's knowledge was no longer a secret. So why continue the association? Such thoughts must have passed through the minds of Hiram and the chief merchant-venturers of Tyre. Although there are slight discrepancies between the two versions of the fitting out of the expedition, as described in the Books of Kings and of Chronicles, they agree entirely that only one combined voyage took place.

The Book of Kings also mentions other voyages to Ophir, but only by Hiram's ships: "And the navy also of Hiram, that brought gold from Ophir, brought in from Ophir great plenty of almug trees, and precious stones." (I Kings 10:11.) The references to Tarshish ships undoubtedly concerned voyages to the city of that name: "For the king's [Solomon's] ships went to Tarshish with the servants of Hiram; every three years once came the ships of Tarshish..." (II Chronicles 9:21.) The voyage to Tarshish and back sometimes lasted three years. The Tyrians probably had a regular service of ships trading the length of the Mediterranean, leaving the home port with products of the Levant and returning with raw materials of the West. Solomon had a considerable share in this trade. His metal industry is believed to have employed eighty thousand men, so production must have been quite high, even allowing for the primitive means of the time. And much of this production was exported in exchange for gold and silver and precious goods, but Phoenician ships did the carrying.

Solomon tried his utmost to build a fleet of his own and to form good crews. No great wisdom was required to realize that the Tyrians would hardly help in the formation of a merchant fleet that was likely to compete with theirs and perhaps oust them altogether from their markets. Tyre had little fear about its position in the Mediterranean trade, but was justifiably apprehensive about the future of its trade with countries south of the Red Sea and across the Indian Ocean. Israel had expanded commercially and industrially, and lacked only a well-equipped fleet to assume control of the Indian Ocean. Unfortunately we have no knowledge of how the situation between the two kingdoms developed. There can be little doubt that Solomon exerted himself to make Israel a maritime power, but he obviously failed to do so. None of his immediate successors appears to have shown the slightest interest in the sea, and no mention can be found of any attempt to build a fleet and train crews. Not until a hundred years after Solomon's death was his throne occupied by a monarch who realized the importance of a fleet and endeavored to create one from scratch. He was King Josaphat, and he must have drawn a lesson from the events of Solomon's reign, for he made no request to Tyre but set about the building of a fleet by his own means. Unfortunately his ships all sank at their moorings before ever getting out to sea, and this so embittered him that he made no further attempt.

If Solomon's efforts to create a navy had been successful, who knows what the history of Israel would have been? As it was, he had obtained great concessions from Hiram, who complied with good grace. Then Solomon ceded twenty towns to Hiram, though it is not known what he received in return, except that Hiram considered himself cheated and made his opinion known, though in a chaffing manner. Despite this and other instances of tricking each other, relations between the two monarchs remained friendly, for each realized that their common interests had to be safeguarded.

Tyre continued to be purely a maritime power and consolidated her position, but Israel neglected the sea after the death of Solomon, and her people turned to the land again. Some modern Hebrew historians nevertheless maintain that the sea has always played a great part in the history of their people, that there was never a time when maritime traditions were lost.

Admittedly, there are many references in the Old Testament to the Hebrews' association with the sea, but this was only natural, for Israel had a coastline even in ancient times. The tribe of Asher in particular, being close to Tyre, produced many good seamen, and there were always some Hebrews in every generation who earned their living from the sea. But this gives no grounds for writing of "a glorious national tradition of the sea." The Hebrews, as a race, certainly did not have the sea in their blood, like truly maritime people. Nor does their literature show much inspiration from the sea. They have always drawn their strength and creative power from the land, which has also determined their political outlook.

In the greatest of Hebrew writings, the Old Testament, the sea is little more than a stage property. The pages are redolent of the desert, the mountaintops and fertile coastal plains. How different, for instance, is the literature of the ancient Greeks— the *Odyssey* smells of brine and seaweed.

The Romans, too, had a coastline, yet never really became a race of seafarers. They had the Etruscans for neighbors, they were in constant contact with the Greeks, they fought the Carthaginians—all seafaring people. But the Romans in general remained aloof from the sea. When they sailed the waters it was from necessity, not inclination.

Modern Israel has her own ships and liners, and many of the younger generation have a deep interest in maritime matters. Young Israelis are being trained as sailors and navigators. That is all to the good, but it is not sufficient basis for the eloquent published writings about "Hebrew maritime history." Some of these writers have even made the assumption, in support of their theories, that the Phoenicians were Hebrews. The Tyrians, they proclaim, were Hebrews, and the Carthaginians too. The language and writing of these people were similar to Hebrew, admittedly; but the manners and customs, the religious beliefs and rites of the Phoenicians were vastly different from those of the Hebrews. The Phoenicians did not believe in one God, and the words of the prophets had no influence upon them. They continued to worship Baal and Astarte, preferring these tangible idols to an invisible God, and their sacrifices to them were usually accompanied by orgiastic rites. The Carthaginians sacrificed human victims—generally babies—to one of their gods, Moloch, who could be appeased only in this way. The unfortunate infants were tied in sacks and grilled over a slow fire, so that the god should be all the more pleased by the smell of roasting flesh. The mothers of the babies were forced to be present at this horrible sacrifice, and were not even supposed to weep, for Moloch did not accept sacrifices which were "drowned in tears." Excavations at Carthage have revealed evidence of terrible holocausts—of more than five hundred children at a time being sacrificed in this manner in time of war, when danger was approaching.

It is not difficult to make a case for the Phoenicians having been Hebrews when one refers only to maritime matters, but when the whole lives and activities of the two peoples are examined it becomes obvious that the Phoenicians had little in common with the children of Israel. Let us render unto the Phoenicians what was Phoenician, and to the Hebrews what was Hebrew . . . and follow the Tyrians on their more ambitious sea voyages.

Whatever may have been the outcome of the royal association of Hiram and Solomon, it is certain that the Phoenicians sailed regularly into the Indian Ocean from that time onward, until the rise of the Persians. It was an important seaway for the Phoenicians, since it took them to countries known to possess great riches, much in demand on the Mediterranean markets. The Phoenician voyages to the East remained shrouded in mystery and silence. They have left very little trace of their presence in the Indian Ocean. Similarly, many centuries later, the Portuguese kept their newly discovered routes to India a close secret.

The Arabian Sea and the ocean to the south hardly ever see mist or fog, and the monsoon winds blow between east Africa and northwest India with a regularity unchanged since time began. From November to March the wind blows steadily from the northeast, while from the end of April to the beginning of October the wind blows from the southwest. The currents of the ocean are controlled by these monsoons. Only during the intermediate periods, when the north and south winds meet and terrific storms arise, is navigation perilous for sailing vessels. But for seamen who know of this exception, the otherwise regular conditions are a great aid to long voyages, and they enable the round trip to be made in a comparatively short time.

The Phoenicians knew about the monsoons, since their ships had sailed to Ophir. Later, they hired out ships and crews to Sennacherib, King of Assyria, when he was trying to gain control of the Persian Gulf. And it was again their ships and seamen that composed Necho's expedition to sail around Africa. The Phoenicians built and navigated a fleet for Darius, too, when he used the seaways to extend his conquests.

According to Indian sources there were regular trade expeditions between India and Assyria during the seventh and sixth centuries B.C., and a part of this trade was in the hands of the Assyrians—in effect, the Phoenicians, as apparently they supplied the ships and crews for the Assyrians and, later, the Babylonians. However, no written record exists to support this surmise.

There is indeed little evidence to support a claim that the Phoenicians sailed the Indian Ocean were it not for the fact that the sailing boats of the natives to those shores are identical, even to this day, with the ships of the Phoenicians. The typical Phoenician ship, as shown on a bas-relief from Sennacherib's palace at Nineveh (now in the British Museum), was exactly like those still seen in Indian waters, around Ceylon and southern India. A similar type of sailing boat is also found along the coast of Senegal and farther south. And evidence exists of Phoenician voyages to Senegal. Was it just by chance that the same type of sailing vessel was found in the Mediterranean, in Scandinavian waters, and along the coasts of Ceylon and of Senegal?

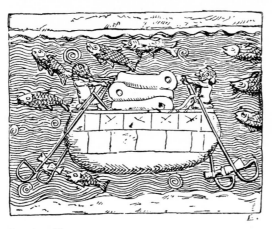

Assyrian ship

Chapter 18

ASSYRIA, A CRUEL EMPIRE

Hiram died after a long, glorious and peaceful reign of nearly thirty-five years. During that time the city of Tyre had greatly developed its trade and increased its prosperity. A tomb recently discovered not far from Tyre is believed by some archaeologists to have been Hiram's; if so, the King's body was not allowed the peace he had worked for in life. The tomb had been desecrated and the remains scattered. The usual curses upon desecrators of tombs, which the Tyrians had adopted from Egyptian customs, had been engraved on a tablet and placed in the sepulcher, but had proved completely ineffective. Either the violators could not read or they were not impressed. Their sole interest was in the treasure buried with the body.

The history of Tyre in the years following Hiram's death is obscure. Kings came and went, and assassination was the order of the day. The only king of whom something is known was Itobaal, or Etbaal, 887–856 B.C., who is mentioned in the Books of Kings and of Chronicles. His reign saw much religious strife. (It was the time of the struggle between monotheism and the worship of Baal.) His daughter Jezebel was married to Ahab, King of Samaria. This was an outstanding period in the history of Tyre, for its people were far more interested in trading than in gaining converts to their religion.

Their prosperity lasted until the end of the ninth century B.C., when the peaceful and untroubled existence of Tyre was

**Ships from Tyre
bringing tribute to
Shalmaneser**

broken by the Assyrians, who were sweeping all before them in
their rise to power.

There is little attractive in the history of the Assyrian empire,
for it was one of militarism and constant acts of cruelty. The two
often go together, but the Assyrians seemed to indulge in
violence for its own sake. They realized that their strength, their
economy and their whole existence depended upon the maintenance of a well-disciplined regular army. They had neither
friends nor allies, and aroused terror and hatred in every land
they invaded. The Assyrians were the first people in history to
have a regular army with specialized branches. The assault force
consisted chiefly of chariots and cavalry, and iron battering rams
were brought up when a town was being besieged. These were
maneuverable and powerful siege machines capable of making
breaches in the thickest walls. The expeditions of the Assyrian
armies were accompanied by terrible atrocities, unsurpassed
even in the Orient. The kings of Assyria recorded their military
acts in great detail, and some of these archives have been
discovered intact and well preserved. They are full of accounts
of destruction and slaughter. Wholesale massacre of vanquished
populations was common practice. Soldiers received a share of
the booty according to the number of prisoners beheaded, often
after they had been blinded or skinned alive. Some Assyrian
kings boasted of having gouged prisoners' eyes out with their
own hands. The list of atrocities is abominable—the cutting off
of nose, ears, and other organs, prisoners crushed under a harrow,
unborn babies torn from their mothers' wombs, children
drowned. Apparently this was part of military science and in
accordance with the Assyrian kings' policy of spreading terror.

160

Never before had such widespread atrocities been committed. The mere mention of the Assyrians was enough to spread panic among a population. A cry of *They are coming!* induced a kind of paralysis which made defensive action impossible. A similar effect was caused, many centuries later, by the approach of the Huns or the Vandals.

The prophet Isaiah vividly described the approach of the dreaded enemy:

" . . . and, behold, they shall come with speed swiftly. None shall be weary nor stumble among them; none shall slumber nor sleep; neither shall the girdle of their loins be loosed, nor the latchet of their shoes be broken.

"Whose arrows are sharp, and all their bows bent, their horses' hoofs shall be counted like flint, and their wheels like a whirlwind. Their roaring shall be like a lion, they shall roar like young lions; yea, they shall roar, and lay hold of the prey, and shall carry it away safe, and none shall deliver it.

Assyrian soldiers crossing river with inflated skin floats

"And in that day they shall roar against them like the roaring of the sea; and if one look unto the land, behold darkness and sorrow, and the light is darkened in the heavens thereof." (Isaiah 5:26–30.)

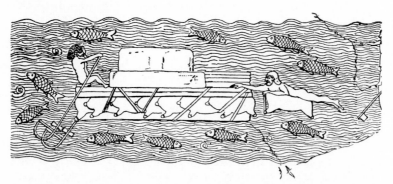

Raft, from relief on palace wall at Nineveh, buoyed up by inflated hides

The Assyrians reached the Mediterranean for the first time about the year 1100 B.C., under Tiglathpileser I. All the Phoenician cities capitulated, preferring to pay the heavy tribute demanded rather than be devastated. But this was only a brief invasion; another two hundred and fifty years passed before the Assyrian kingdom was strongly established and militarily capable of sustained aggressive action in the direction of the Mediterranean. In the middle of the ninth century B.C. King Assurnazirpal repeated Tiglathpileser's campaign. The cruelty and sadism of this monarch remained unparalleled in history until modern times, when Hitler and his Nazis invented methods of mass killings. The Phoenician cities again submitted without a fight; Tyre, Sidon, Gebal, and Arvad escaped destruction by paying heavy taxes.

During the reign of Assurnazirpal's son some of the inland towns, Damascus and Hamath prominent among them, united in a revolt against the common enemy, but they were soon forced to capitulate. The conquered seaboard cities continued to pay taxes to Nineveh, and thereby obtained a certain amount of autonomy and fairly extensive trading rights. The taxes were paid in gold and silver, bronze or tin, in timber, clothing, purple cloth and ivory. Peace was bought at a heavy cost, and it lasted for one hundred and fifty years. Throughout that period the Phoenicians refused to join the Egyptians against the Assyrians, although the former's agents were constantly inciting the Phoenicians to revolt and promising them the earth. But Tyre and the other cities were not to be tempted. They knew that Egypt was prepared to fight Assyria to the last soldier—the last foreign soldier. Moreover, the comparative calm had certain

162

advantages. Overland trade routes were safe from attack, and the Assyrians did not interfere with the Phoenicians' sea-trading. In fact Tyre and the other cities seem to have known real prosperity while under Assyrian domination.

"... she is a mart of nations; ... Tyre, the crowning city, whose merchants are princes, whose traffickers are the honorable of the earth." So wrote Isaiah, when he predicted the overthrow of Tyre.

This peaceful period was disrupted in the latter part of the eighth century B.C. when Shalmaneser V, son of Tiglathpileser the Great, came to the Assyrian throne. He reigned only five years, from 727 to 722 B.C., and did little more than conduct military expeditions, one of which was directed against Tyre.

Nothing is known of the reasons for this sudden deterioration in relations between Tyre and Nineveh. The former may have tried to throw off a yoke which seemed likely to become heavier. In any case, Shalmaneser's expedition was brutal and bloody in the extreme. Other Phoenician cities opened their gates to the Assyrian, for they had no time in which to prepare for a siege. Tyre alone defied the enemy force. Shalmaneser was able to capture the old town on the mainland, but failed to take the island city. He had no fleet, and throughout the siege Tyre easily kept her sea communications open.

Shalmaneser later led another army into Phoenicia, and again Tyre was the only city to close its gates to him. So the Assyrian king decided to make an example of the Tyrians, to punish them in such a way that it would be a memorable lesson to the other Phoenician cities. The latter were ordered to supply him with a fleet of sixty warships, for he intended making a surprise attack on Tyre, most of whose ships were then in distant waters. But he obtained only a dozen ships, and the Tyrians succeeded in beating off the attack. They even captured five hundred Assyrians, according to Flavius Josephus. However, Shalmaneser then laid siege to Tyre from the mainland, and for five years the island city was threatened by the enemy across the narrow channel. The Tyrians were soon without drinking water—the wells were on the mainland—and had to rely on rainwater caught in barrels and ditches. Then the Assyrian king died, and national strife caused the army to raise the siege and return to Nineveh.

The succeeding kings, Sargon and then Sennacherib, attacked Phoenician cities on more than one occasion, but Tyre's resistance and unshakable determination in the face of Shalmaneser's army had not been forgotten, and that city was

163

left in peace. The Tyrians still had to pay taxes to the Assyrians, but benefited from special trading rights as in the past. The pride of the Assyrian kings was satisfied, while Tyre continued in all tranquillity to accumulate wealth from her commercial activities. This situation kept everyone happy.

Sennacherib was succeeded by Esar-Haddon, who reigned from 688 to 668 B.C. At that time Tyre and the whole of Phoenicia were ruled by a monarch named Baal. He raised the standard of revolt against the Assyrians—encouraged, it seems, by the Egyptians—and the consequence was not long in coming. Esar-Haddon invaded Phoenicia at the head of a large army, devastating the countryside and putting populations to the sword. The seaboard towns again capitulated without a fight, and were spared destruction by payment of huge tributes. Tyre was again the exception, and endured another siege; it ended after four years, at the death of the Assyrian king.

**Assyrian soldiers
pursuing the enemy
across a river**

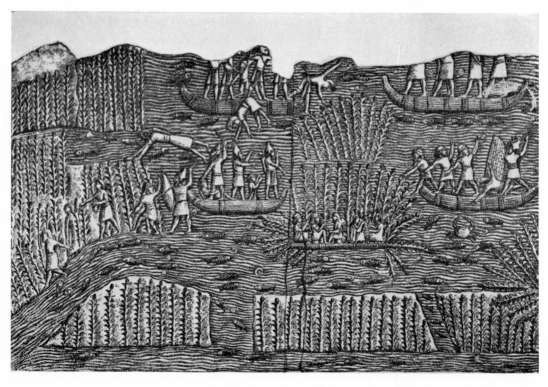

Lion-hunting in the marshes of Assyria from a large boat of Tyrean design

Esar-Haddon had intended to attack Egypt, but either his death came too soon or the determined resistance of Tyre upset his plans. As for the Tyrians, the siege had not unduly affected their trading activities overseas. Their king did not neglect, however, to take many gifts to Esar-Haddon's successor, Assurbanipal. This monarch boasted that twenty-one kings—most of them from Phoenicia and Israel—came to "kiss the soles of his feet." His rule proved to be so hard and cruel that the Phoenician cities revolted yet again, with the same result as before. Tyre alone held out against Assurbanipal, who had soon acquired a reputation for bloodthirstiness even worse than any of his predecessors.

A surprising aspect of these periodic revolts of the Phoenicians is that, confronted with such a powerful and terrible enemy, they seem never to have thought of combining their strength. The fighting force of each city-kingdom obviously had no chance, independently, against the well-trained, "mechanized" battalions of the Assyrian army. The maxim, in union there is

165

strength, appears to have been unknown to the Phoenicians, and they paid the consequences. Tyre alone succeeded in resisting the enemy, because of her geographical position and large fleet.

On the other hand, Assyria was weakened by being almost perpetually at war, not only against the Phoenicians but all the peoples of the Orient. After the death of Assurbanipal in 626 B.C. the decline of the Assyrian empire began and rapidly increased. At the same time a new and vigorous dynasty appeared in Babylonia. It was founded by the Chaldaean Nabopolasser, who waged war against Assyria with his Median ally. By 612 B.C. the two chief cities of Assyria, Nineveh and Assur, had been captured and laid waste. The country ceased to exist as a political power.

The Assyrian kings had captured and devastated thousands of towns in their time. When Xenophon and his Ten Thousand made their great forced march back to Greece, in 401 B.C., they passed over the ground where Nineveh had stood. They were unaware that they were treading on the ruins of a city that, little more than two hundred years earlier, had still been dominating the Orient after four centuries of power and whose name alone had been enough to set people trembling with fear.

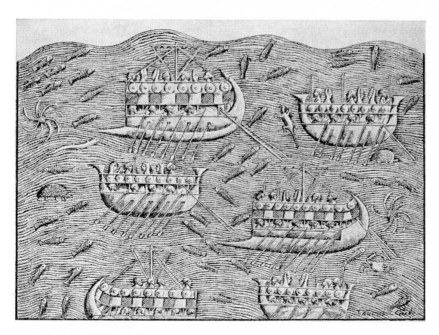

**The fleet of Sennacherib:
all vessels of
Phoenician build**

"THE TRAFFICKERS OF THE EARTH"

After the fall of Assyria a new period of great prosperity opened for Tyre. She became completely independent and enjoyed much prestige for her repeated, heroic stands against the cruel Assyrian kings. Proud and rich, and with a glorious past, the chief Phoenician city dominated the world of business and trade. Carthage was by then well established, powerful and wealthy too, but in no way competed with Tyre. Rather, Carthage complemented the mother city on the world's markets, and remained as loyal as a devoted daughter should be.

An authentic commentary on Tyre at this period can be found in the Book of Ezekiel (Chapters 26–28). The prophet had no particular reason for looking kindly upon Tyre, whose people had exclaimed with joy on learning of the destruction of Jerusalem by Nebuchadnezzar. They had good cause to rejoice, for a great rival had thus been eradicated. The Tyrians supplied the slave markets of various countries with Judeans captured by the Babylonians; and the perfect accord which had lasted for so long was broken by the Phoenicians.

It was but natural for the prophet Ezekiel to predict the fall of Tyre. "Great waters shall cover thee," he announced. Ezekiel

167

was well aware of the high place Tyre held among the nations as a center of trade, and his admiration for the Phoenician city, whose beauty he appreciated, emerges from his writing. "Thy borders are in the midst of the seas, thy builders have perfected thy beauty." The temples of Tyre, the sanctuaries and even the statues were covered with precious stones; evidence of great wealth was everywhere. And in addition, wrote the prophet, Tyre was a center of wisdom.

The power of Tyre was drawn from the sea, and her people were expert at building ships, for which they used the very best and most expensive materials:

"They have made all thy ship boards of fir trees of Senir; they have taken cedars from Lebanon to make masts for thee. Of the oaks of Bashan have they made thine oars; the company of the Ashurites have made thy benches of ivory, brought out of the isles of Chittim." (Ezekiel 27:5, 6.)

And Ezekiel went on to give an example of the splendor of Tyrian ships—the sails were made of "fine linen with broidered work from Egypt," and they were dyed "blue and purple from the isles of Elishah." Egyptian linen was so costly that usually only priests could afford to have garments made of it.

"Situated at the entry of the sea," Tyre was destined to be "a merchant of the people for many isles"—in other words, to be the commercial agent and middleman, the trafficker (as the Old Testament has it), between the mainland and the islands of the Mediterranean. Tyre had a large fleet of fine, swift ships. All their captains were Tyrians, Ezekiel tells us, but most of the crews came from other Phoenician towns: "The inhabitants of Sidon and Arvad were thy mariners; thy wise men, O Tyrus, that were in thee, were thy pilots." The ship-repairers were specialists from another town: "The ancients of Gebal and the wise men thereof were in thee thy calkers; all the ships of the sea with their mariners were in thee to occupy thy merchandise." The people of Gebal had a long tradition of shipbuilding; craftsmen and skilled workers from several Phoenician towns found employment and refuge in Tyre. Ezekiel exaggerates in saying that all the ships sailing the seas were Tyrian, but so great was the renown of Tyre that the prophet can be excused. His words, nevertheless, underline the fact that the Tyrian fleet was much larger than any other and indeed held command of the seaways.

Ezekiel also gave much information about the trading activities and markets of Tyre. The ships brought cargoes of "silver, iron, tin, and lead" from Tarshish. Tyre held the monopoly of trade with the tin islands (southwest England), and imported vast

168

Phoenician war galley

quantities of wheat, linen, cotton and papyrus from Egypt, while Greece and the coastal areas of Asia Minor supplied "vessels of brass, purple, and broidered work . . . and the persons of men [slaves]." The many warrior tribes of Asia Minor kept the slave markets well supplied. In addition, the Tyrians were not above making sudden raids on coastal settlements to obtain human merchandise. Slaves from the northern Mediterranean lands were shipped to Egypt, Arabia, and Assyria, while those from southern lands were sold in the international market on the Aegean island of Delos. The Tyrians also shipped cedar from Lebanon and from Cyprus, and supplied many European countries with rare skins, ivory, ebony, colored plumes and precious stones from Africa and India. And, of course, they exported Phoenician products, notably purple cloth, glassware, jewelry and bronze articles. It can be seen how great and varied the trading activities of the Tyrians were, and what huge profits they must have made.

These activities were not confined to the seaways. They had caravans carrying goods overland, too, trading particularly with the tribes of Israel. "Judah, and the land of Israel, they were thy merchants; they traded in thy market wheat of Minnith, and honey, and oil, and balm." Aram sold rich apparel, embroidery and carpets to the Tyrians, and Damascus sold them "the wine of Helbon, and white wool," while "they of the house of Togarmah traded in thy fairs with horses and horsemen and mules." Togarmah was Anatolia, which was famed for horse breeding, then as now. The Tyrians had captured the market in horses and mules from the Hebrews, buying whole herds in Anatolia and selling them in Egypt and other southern countries. Saddles and decorated harness were obtained in Arabia, as well as riding clothes, which were a specialty of that region. The Tyrians had for many generations been buying goats and rams there, too. Arab caravans brought their riches to Tyrian markets: "The merchants of Sheba and Raamah, they were thy merchants; they occupied in thy fairs with chief of all spices, and with all precious stones, and gold." The Tyrians employed Arab caravans to import the famous perfumes of southern Arabia and even of India, and other rare products came overland from countries bordering the Indian Ocean. The jewelry trade of Tyre, which had developed considerably, was always in need of metals and precious stones. And, to complete the list of goods and products negotiated by the Tyrians in this overland commerce, there were the spices from the Far East. For many centuries longer the people of Europe regarded spices as one of the luxuries of life. Two thousand years after the fall of Tyre, the European explorers who set out to discover the spice route reached "unknown" countries with which the Phoenicians of Tyre and Sidon had been familiar.

The long list of Eastern countries with which the Tyrians traded is most impressive: Assyria, Persia, Dedan, Javan, Arabia, Kedar, Haran, Aden, etc. The identity of some is still a matter of controversy. But there is no doubt that Tyre had trade relations with practically every country of the known world of the time. Much organization was obviously necessary, and the Tyrians preferred to use the seaways whenever possible. This was natural enough, as they were a maritime people, but from a commercial point of view transport by ship was cheaper, faster, and safer than by caravan. The dangers at sea were fewer than those on land. However, the Tyrians had to keep open the caravan routes to inland countries. In order to reach Nineveh or Babylon a caravan from Tyre had to pass through a number of hostile lands and regions where the people lived largely from attacking and plundering merchant caravans. The risks were great—but worth taking.

170

The caravans usually had an escort of soldiers, and the merchants were armed and ready to help beat off an attack— or to buy protection. In fact they preferred to pay for the safe transit of their caravans, as this arrangement enabled them to make regular journeys and keep their clients satisfied. The tribes soon realized, too, that it was preferable to accept "passage money" than to fight for it. And so the caravan routes became relatively safe and the arrival of merchandise dependable. The Tyrians probably had to pay heavily, but it was part of the cost and the customer—then as now—paid in the end. Perhaps the merchants even made a little on that too.

The caravan routes to the north, to Anatolia and Armenia (the "Van" or "Urmia" of Hittite writings), were long and difficult, traversing mountainous regions where snow lay all the year. The Tyrians, more used to the Mediterranean warmth, suffered much from the hardness of the climate, but they had great stamina and were not people to be dismayed by accidents and misadventures. They adapted themselves to conditions in the highlands, and in time became adept at picking out mountain paths and getting their pack mules—and human porters too— over the high passes.

What excitement the arrival of a Phoenician caravan must have caused among the wild tribes of Armenia, Turkestan, or eastern Anatolia. Imagine the lively, noisy scene when the traders from the West displayed their wares in the marketplace. Money was unknown, bartering was the order of the day. The natives offered chiefly horses and mules, and iron bars; many tribes were in the habit of selling girls too. The scene must have been most picturesque, with the gesturing and haggling—for what indeed was the equivalent in goods of a horse or a young virgin?

The return journey with herds of half-tamed horses, over the mountains, was obviously one full of danger, calling for skill and great determination. In truth, the Phoenicians did not choose the easiest means of acquiring wealth.

By opening up and maintaining regular trade communications with the peoples of the Middle East, the Phoenicians undoubtedly had a civilizing effect upon them, and spread knowledge and ideas over a wide area. As well they marked out overland routes that supplemented the seaways.

Assyria had been eliminated as a power, and Babylonia was still preparing fresh aggression. During this interim period Tyre was the commercial and diplomatic center of the ancient world, and a dominating influence along overland routes and seaways. The great powers regarded her with envy.

171

Babylon:
the Ishtar Gate

Chapter 20

THE BABYLONIAN SIEGE OF TYRE

Egypt was suddenly roused from lethargy, impelled by the native Saite pharaohs, especially the energetic and ambitious Psammetichus and his son Necho II. The old toothless lion gathered strength for a last leap. Necho led an army north, as in the good old days. Judah was conquered and the Phoenician cities capitulated without a fight, preferring to pay tribute in order to continue their trading activities unmolested.

The Egyptian recovery was brief, for the Babylonian star had already risen in the East. With their Median allies, the Babylonians crushed the Assyrians and captured Nineveh in 612 B.C. Nebuchadnezzar, the son of the Babylonian king, then led the armies against Egyptian forces, which were supported by those of Judah and Phoenicia, and utterly defeated them. But he was unable to follow up his victory and invade Egypt, for the

173

death of his father, Nabopolassar, caused him to return to Babylon to claim the throne. However, Nebuchadnezzar did not forget that Judah and the Phoenician cities had supported the Egyptian cause, and he realized that in order to strengthen his authority over his realm a sound lesson had to be dealt to those tiny kingdoms, and especially to his chief enemy, Egypt.

Assyrian cavalry attacking

Several years passed before Nebuchadnezzar's military preparations were complete. The intelligence services of the Phoenicians and the Judeans could not have been very good, or else they put too much faith in Egypt and the slight information grudgingly handed out from that source. There seems no other explanation for all the peoples of the Middle East suddenly rising in revolt against Babylon, whose rule was lighter and more humane than that of Nineveh had been, and with whom an arrangement could easily have been reached. The blind attachment of these people to the Egyptian cause is difficult to understand. The reasons for it remain one of the great mysteries of history. The prophets were well aware that Egypt was "a broken reed"; and the kings of Judah, as well as the Phoenician potentates, had often been disillusioned by the failure of the Egyptians to respect their treaty obligations. Aged empires have never been eager to take up arms. But they excel at political intrigue, at playing off one nation against another. The leaders of Judah and Phoenicia were taken in by the soft words and promises of the Egyptians.

Meanwhile, Nebuchadnezzar had gathered and trained an army of more than one hundred thousand foot soldiers, one hundred and twenty thousand horsemen and ten thousand chariots. And the day came when this vast force moved to the

174

attack "like a great whirlwind raised up from the coasts of the earth." Sidon surrendered without striking a blow. Gebal, Arvad, and Acre were quick to pay tribute and to acknowledge the authority of Babylon. Jerusalem was captured and destroyed after a siege which lasted two years. Tyre was the only city still to hold out against the aggressor. Cut off from the rest of the world, abandoned by her Egyptian allies, Tyre withstood the siege for five years. Then the mainland town fell, and the vengeance of Nebuchadnezzar was terrible. The wrath of this oriental despot against a small town that had dared resist his incomparable army for five years can be imagined. The captured town was pillaged and destroyed. Apart from the few who managed to reach the island city, all the inhabitants were put to the sword—for Nebuchadnezzar never boasted of having taken any prisoners into captivity.

But the island city continued to hold out—for thirteen years in all. Nebuchadnezzar employed every military means of the time to reduce the fortified city, but without success. The Phoenician cities which had surrendered were ordered to assemble their ships in one great fleet and send it against Tyre, but this attempt failed too. The beleaguered city nevertheless

Akkadian seal

suffered much from the enemy siege machines, the iron battering rams and the great catapults, and the inhabitants were often almost without food or drinking water. Their ships were attacked by those of other Phoenician cities, and only a few succeeded now and again in slipping through the blockade and bringing supplies to the besieged Tyrians.

In the end, Nebuchadnezzar raised the siege on certain conditions—or perhaps Tyre surrendered on honorable terms. All

175

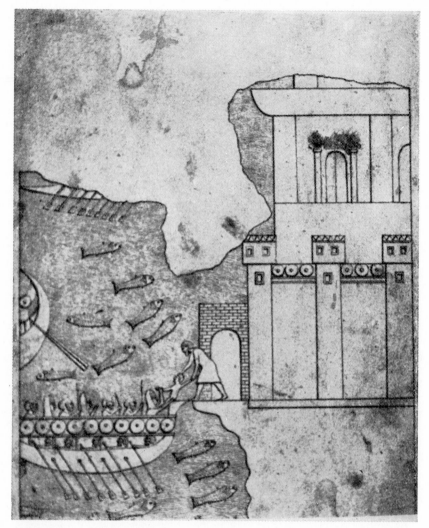

After the siege:
the Assyrian Army
taking prisoners aboard
Phoenician ships

is conjecture, for no record has ever been found of the final events in this siege, justly considered one of the longest known to history. It is highly unlikely, though, that the all-conquering Nebuchadnezzar, master of all lands from Persia to the Mediterranean, folded his tents and crept away after trying for thirteen years to capture the city of Tyre—which was really no more than a fly, albeit a tough fly, irritating the Babylonian lion. Throughout his long life, Nebuchadnezzar was always ready to lead a punitive expedition against a town or tribe in revolt in any part of his wide realm. In any case, Tyre was not plundered at the end of the siege, nor were the inhabitants harmed or sent

176

PLATE 10

Ship of Sidon, about the third century B.C.

Designed and built by M. Pliner from a carved marble sarcophagus of the third century B.C., found in the old harbor at Sidon.

At this period, and indeed for long afterward in the Roman period, it was customary to represent on the sides of the sarcophagus events from the life of the person who had commissioned its making, though, in fact, the original occupant might, in time, be replaced and the interior filled with the remains of his successor.

There is, therefore, nothing surprising in finding a slightly ornamental sarcophagus on the bottom of the harbor at Sidon, covered with carvings which represent in some detail a type of ship characteristic of this period. It is primarily, indeed exclusively, a sailing ship. The mainsail is square in shape, but so rigged as to be capable of moving around the mast in a very large segment. There is also a foresail on a foremast which is heavily raked forward, for auxiliary use. The structure seems to be reinforced with cables in the ancient manner. The sternpost is carved in a swan's-neck pattern, this bird having become a favorite symbolic design with seagoing adventurers at this period.

The sarcophagus was discovered in 1914 by the French archaeologist M. Contenau.

PLATE 10

Ship of Sidon, about the third century B.C.

into exile, whereas other cities, which had offered little resistance to the Babylonians, had been punished in a ferocious manner.

It is possible that both sides grew weary of the struggle. A considerable part of the Babylonian army had been tied down for thirteen years, and for reasons of prestige a compromise solution had to be found. Some arrangement was obviously reached, whereby Nebuchadnezzar saved face and the Tyrians their lives and property.

The long struggle had nevertheless been ruinous for the island city. Its trading activities had dwindled almost to nothing during the last years of the siege, and what remained of its fleet was in bad shape. From an economic standpoint, the resistance to the Babylonians had been a great mistake. But the Tyrians had again proved that—contrary to tales spread by the Greeks and accepted by other people—they were capable of heroic exploits such as few populations in history have equaled. Their love of liberty and spirit of independence were stronger than their commercial instincts. Though they were seafarers and traders, when the occasion demanded they showed fighting qualities that were on a par with the courage needed for their intrepid voyages.

The scars left by the siege were a long time in healing, and the eminent position of Tyre among the Phoenician cities was for a period taken over by Sidon. It should have been obvious to the Phoenicians, after all they had endured at the hands of the Assyrians and the Babylonians, that no one city, however rich and steadfast, could hope to emerge victorious from a lone struggle against the might of a great power. Yet they still refused to draw the logical conclusion and to unite. Each city continued to maintain its autonomy. They did, however, generally resolve to keep out of quarrels and wars between the great powers in the future, and when strife again broke out between Babylonia and Egypt the Phoenician cities observed a strict neutrality. They had learned that it was wiser to wait and see how the struggle developed before taking sides.

Actually, the domination of Babylon did not weigh heavily upon the Phoenicians. The taxes levied by the Babylonian kings were not excessive, and in return the Phoenician cities were granted many trading privileges. Their internal affairs were left in their own hands, and no pressure was brought to bear upon their religious practices. So it is not surprising that the Phoenicians remained faithful to Babylon almost until her fall. During the half-century that elapsed between the great siege of Tyre and the fall of Babylon, all the Phoenician cities were able to redevelop their trade and increase the size of their fleets, building a new and better type of vessel. The terrible experiences of the past had convinced them that, in a struggle against a great power, their only hope was to have a strong fleet. The action of Phoenician ships was in fact the one means of exercising pressure upon an aggressor and of obtaining privileges and concessions from a powerful neighbor.

Lydian coins

Chapter 21

PERSIA, GREATEST OF ALL KINGDOMS

In the sixth century B.C. a new power appeared upon the scene. The Persians were a hardy mountain race and had been battling for centuries to maintain their independence against the Assyrians and the Babylonians. When Cyrus came to the throne he found himself at the head of a strong, courageous army eager for combat and conquest.

Cyrus was not only a great soldier, but a skillful politician and an outstanding organizer as well. He taught his doughty mountain warriors the use of new weapons and trained them into a disciplined force. He then conquered the neighboring country of Media, had himself proclaimed King of the Medes and Persians, and proceeded next to invade Lydia—which bordered his new realm to the west—in pursuance of his grandiose aim to make himself master of the whole of the Middle East.

Sardes, the capital of Lydia, was famous for its great wealth, and King Croesus was said to be the richest man in the world. His wealth came from the flourishing trade of the country, from levies on all the caravans which passed through his territory, and from taxes on the Greek merchants using his ports. Cyrus made a surprise attack on Lydia, and Croesus took refuge within the massive walls of his capital, which was believed to be

179

impregnable. But Cyrus captured it after a siege of only a fortnight, and all the wealth of Croesus did not save him from being condemned to be burnt alive.

A legend relates how he was saved from the flames at the last minute.

When Solon of Athens, one of the Seven Sages, went on his travels he was received at the court of Croesus, who showed Solon his treasures and all the evident affluence of his land. In common with most rich men, Croesus was very vain. Having shown off his possessions, he asked Solon to name the happiest man he had ever known. The proud monarch was surprised and annoyed by his guest's reply, for Solon merely said: "The gods give men a glimmer of happiness, which leads them on to perdition. Call no man happy till he is dead." Solon dropped considerably in the king's estimation, for Croesus could not understand why the wise man placed so little importance on material wealth. Years later, Croesus was greatly saddened by the death of his son in a hunting accident. Then the Delphic oracle foretold that if Croesus fought Persia a great empire would be destroyed. This double-edged prophecy was amply fulfilled. When his kingdom was overthrown, his family wiped out, and he himself about to be burnt alive, Croesus remembered Solon's words. At last he understood their meaning, and called out, "Solon! Solon! Solon!" Cyrus heard the cry and asked for an explanation. On being told, he ordered the King of Lydia to be released, and Croesus became his loyal adviser.

Coin of the time of Croesus

Cyrus, unlike other Eastern rulers, neither destroyed nor plundered captured cities, nor did he massacre their inhabitants. Whether this was due to the counsels of Croesus or to his own instincts is a matter of conjecture. In any case, this policy was amply justified by results. The conquered peoples became part of the Persian realm, continuing to work unmolested but paying a proportion of their earnings to the Persians. The treasures they had accumulated in the past were kept intact to swell Cyrus' own wealth.

Babylonia was the next country to be attacked by the Persians. The Phoenicians maintained a strict neutrality, and seized the opportunity to throw off the Babylonian yoke when the complete victory of Cyrus was seen to be imminent. In 539 B.C. the conquering armies of Cyrus the Great marched into Babylon.

The action of the Phoenician cities had not passed unnoticed by Cyrus. As they had been dependents of the Babylonian empire they should have passed to the new ruler. However, Cyrus took no immediate action against them, being well aware

Croesus on his
funeral pyre

that before long they would ask to be placed under his protection and authority.

The Greeks had become powerful trade rivals of the Phoenicians. They had established themselves along the coast of Asia Minor—Herodotus wrote of Miletus (founded by Athens) as the glory of Ionia and the rival of Tyre—and it was therefore in the Phoenician interest to expel them. But this was possible only with the help of a great power. The Phoenicians made approaches to Cyrus and were taken under his wing. He had come up against the Greeks of Asia Minor on several occasions during his occupation of Lydia.

Although the enormous wealth of Babylon fell into the hands of Cyrus, the ancient city was not harmed and remained a center of learning and industry. Egypt alone was still independent. Moreover, she continued to oppose Persia, probably not realizing the strength of this new empire. The pharaoh Amasis, for instance, claimed Cyprus on the grounds that the island had formerly been part of the Egyptian empire.

In 529 B.C. Cyrus was killed in a battle against the Scythians, leaving to his son Cambyses a vast realm extending from India to the Mediterranean. In spite of the many wars, it was a well-organized empire, divided into separate provinces each with

181

its own governor. Transport and the collection of taxes and postal communications all functioned well, and the army was highly trained and disciplined.

The Persians, however, had no interest in maritime matters, and were scornful even of river navigation. It was said that Cyrus, the victor of so many battles, halted his army whenever he came to a river and so allowed his enemies to escape. They naturally took to boats, rafts, or any other means of reaching the opposite bank.

Cambyses was as skillful a general as his father. He realized that to conquer Egypt he would need a powerful fleet to attack the Delta while his army was pushing inland. Ships were essential for his lines of communication, too, for keeping his armies supplied and maintaining control of the eastern Mediterranean. The answer to his problems lay with the merchant-venturers of Sidon and Tyre, who had all the ships and crews that Cambyses needed.

Nothing is known of the negotiations between Cambyses and the Phoenicians, but had force been employed, history would have made mention of it. Cambyses probably just offered them a large bribe.

So the campaign against Egypt was good business for the Phoenicians. Cambyses had no lack of money, and the Phoenicians were always open to the kind of argument he put forward. He probably offered other advantages too. The Phoenician cities continued to pay light taxes to the Persians, which exempted them from military service and from contributing to the maintenance of the army. They had almost complete autonomy. In addition, the Persian royal navy was to be under the command of a Phoenician, and Phoenician ships were to lead it. But even without these concessions it is unlikely that the Phoenicians would have hesitated to align themselves with the Persians in a campaign directed against the Greeks, their rivals, who were firmly established in the Delta.

This alliance so impressed the Cypriots that their ships abandoned the Egyptian cause and went over to the Persians. The fleet at the disposal of Cambyses was large enough to crush the Egyptian naval forces in one brief engagement. Persian troops occupied towns in the Delta and invaded Memphis, to which the Egyptians had retreated in the hope of defying the invader from behind its strong fortifications. But the well-trained and disciplined Persians soon captured the Egyptian capital. And so Egypt passed into Persian hands. The oldest and most cultivated empire of the ancient world had fallen in a

182

Lydian ornament

very short time before the combination of Phoenician ships and Persian military strength. Cambyses ruled over a great empire— the land and sea communications of the Middle East and the eastern Mediterranean were all under his control. Unlike previous conquerors, however, the Persians pursued an enlightened policy. This was not entirely altruistic. The "great kings" of Persia and their advisers had a keen sense of business, and drew the utmost profit from overland trade, while sharing with the Phoenicians the benefits from maritime trade. Although the Persians were never seafarers they well understood the importance of controlling a fleet of ships. At this period in history, sea power was having an increasing influence upon the conduct of military operations, and therefore upon the fate of many peoples. The coexistence of the Persian empire and the Phoenician cities is quite understandable, for there was a strong basis of common interests.

The Persians were as jealous of their political and military strength as the Phoenicians were of their commercial power. For by the fifth century B.C., Tyre and Sidon were no longer the only great maritime cities. Carthage was at the height of her power, and some of the permanent Greek settlements had greatly increased their spheres of influence. Carthage remained loyal to Tyre and cooperated with the founder city, but the Greeks, those daring seafarers and keen traders, were dangerous rivals. A major clash between them and the Perso-Phoenician alliance appeared inevitable.

After the conquest of Egypt, Cambyses "held council with himself," as Herodotus ironically put it, and decided to prepare three military attacks. One was against Carthage, although there

183

seems no reason for it—unless the "folly of greatness" of the Persian kings, drunk with success, was already showing itself. In any case, Cambyses gave orders for troops to embark and the ships to sail for Carthage. The Phoenicians thus found themselves in a delicate situation, faced with the alternative of attacking a sister city or disobeying the all-powerful monarch. Should they follow the dictates of conscience or risk incurring the wrath of Cambyses? He could easily bring about the collapse of the whole economy of Tyre and Sidon.

The Phoenicians chose the path of honor and refused to sail against Carthage. And the reaction of the Persian king was no less surprising. He not only accepted the refusal but made no retaliation for this blow to his prestige and authority. He thus gave proof of his political wisdom. The understanding he had shown drew the Phoenicians closer to the Persian cause, and they remained faithful allies for one hundred and fifty years. They took part in all the naval battles of the Persians, and submitted to the heavy taxation resulting from the wars. Cambyses was not so unintelligent as Greek historians have tried to make out.

Under his successor, Darius, Persian civilization reached its peak. Darius had fine roads built, organized a postal service for official use, and introduced a coinage system for the whole of his realm. The Phoenician cities naturally profited from this administrative progress and the favorable economic situation.

The long struggle between the Persians and the Greeks was fought out almost entirely at sea, or by naval forces supporting the military. Most of the ships on the Persian side were Phoenician, and were, in general, better vessels with more experienced captains and crews than those of their Greek opponents. An interesting description of a Phoenician ship was given by the Greek historian Xenophon; he went aboard and was greatly surprised to find how well equipped she was. "The ship was armed with a number of destructive weapons for attacking enemy vessels, and carried arms for the crew. Moreover, there were all the utensils needed for the cooking of meals. And the ship was loaded with goods on which the owner [or captain] made a profit." Xenophon admired the neat manner in which the cargo was stowed; everything was in its place— equipment, goods, weapons. He quoted the captain's reply when Xenophon asked him why he kept inspecting the hold, the equipment and the rigging: "Stranger, I make sure that all is in order on board, that nothing is missing. For you can't worry about what is missing when a storm gets up, and there's no time

184

then to stow things as they ought to be." The words of this old sea dog are just as valid today.

Despite the superiority of the Phoenician ships and crews, however, the Persians failed to destroy the Greeks, and after the defeat of Xerxes, the son of Darius, at the naval battle of Salamis, the Persians were obliged to withdraw to the mainland of Asia. The Greeks were fighting for an ideal, for a way of life. They were prepared to die rather than lose their freedom. This was an incalculable factor in the victory of the Greeks over the Persians.

Lydian coin

Head of column from Persepolis

Chapter 22

TWO CURIOUS EXPEDITIONS

Two accounts by Herodotus of exploration by sea indicate the interests of the Persians in this matter. Darius I sent a Greek (or Carian) named Scylax, with other trusted persons, to explore the river Indus to its mouth and then to coast along the shores westward. Avoiding the Persian Gulf, which the Persians knew enough about already, he was to sail around unknown Arabia into the Red Sea and so to Egypt, which they still held. Entering the Indus from the Kabul River, Scylax and his companions carried out their mission and after two and a half years' adventurous voyaging, and doubtless trading, came to a point near the modern Suez. Such is the extent of Herodotus's account. Because of the lack of details, and the absence of travelers' stories which usually spice the pages of Herodotus, doubts have been thrown upon the reality of the voyage. Why should Darius send a Greek mariner, when those of Tyre and Sidon were so loyal to him? The Phoenicians had a high reputation for intrepid sea voyages, and the Persians had in all probability heard of their circumnavigation of Africa.

According to Herodotus, Scylax sailed from east to west, whereas it would have been more logical to explore from west to east. And the time taken by the expedition, two and a half years, seems overlong. Nevertheless, the evidence of those who doubt is entirely negative. The voyage apparently did take place,

187

King Darius I

and was the beginning of the exploration of the Erythraean Sea (the name given by the ancients to the waters between Africa and the northwest coast of India).

Scylax set sail about the year 510 B.C., long before the wars between Persia and the Greeks, so there was nothing remarkable in Darius's calling upon the services of a Greek. In fact, many Greek traders were then venturing into the Red Sea on Darius's behalf. Scylax probably began his voyage in the east because the western parts of India were held by the Persians. The length of time taken might well have been due to his being delayed by an adverse monsoon, as well as by trading, or exploring the possibilities of trading, at the ports along his route. As a result, Darius made use of Indian waters, and probably reopened the old canal between the Nile and the Red Sea. A hieroglyphic inscription of Persian date found along this canal route says: "it is possible for ships to sail direct from the Nile to Persia by way of Saba."

The prophecy about the canal made during the reign of Necho—whose brainchild it had been—had come true. The greatest use of it was being made by Egypt's enemies.

Although Herodotus has little to say about Scylax's expedition, he gives many travelers' tales about the Indus district. The inhabitants had to pay large sums in gold to their Persian conquerors, and the precious metal was fetched from afar— beyond the country of the "Bachians" and the "Pachians," where there was apparently a great desert infested with antlike animals. According to Herodotus, they were larger than foxes and lived in burrows which were filled with gold, for the sands of the desert contained pure gold. The native Indians collected

188

this precious sand in the heat of the day, when the "gold-ant" was sheltering from the fierce sun. By the time the animals roused up again, the robbers were a long way off—fortunately for them, as the ants were said to be very agile and savage creatures.

This story of the gold-ant was handed down over the centuries and caught the imagination of treasure-seekers. In the course of time the animals were credited with further attributes. In the twelfth century A.D. Prester John, who founded a Christian kingdom in Ethiopia, maintained that they had seven legs and four wings. The native Indians must have been smart to escape from such well-equipped monsters. And as late as the sixteenth century it was said that the Shah of Persia sent a gift of several gold-ants to Suleiman the Great, but they never became acclimatized to Constantinople and refused to make anthills packed with gold.

The other account of Persian exploration given by Herodotus is more engaging than the first, and is written in his usual bantering style. This voyage was undertaken in the time of King Xerxes (485–465 B.C.), under the leadership of a Persian of the royal house named Sataspes, who was probably a cousin of Xerxes. Sataspes had committed a shameful act upon a girl over whom the king had exclusive rights. Any ordinary person would have been executed out of hand, but a member of the royal family was entitled to favorable treatment even in Persia. In expiation of his wicked deed Sataspes was ordered to sail around Africa, starting from Egypt and passing through the Pillars of Hercules.

So Sataspes went to Egypt, and having taken a ship and engaged a crew in the Delta—Herodotus does not say whether they were Phoenicians or Greeks—he sailed westward through the Mediterranean. Beyond Gibraltar he "sailed toward the south, but having crossed over much sea in many months, and because there was ever need of more and more voyaging, he turned and sailed back to Egypt." Herodotus explains that he feared the length of the voyage and the loneliness of it, so he did not accomplish the task laid upon him. "And coming thence to King Xerxes' court, he told him that at the farthest point of his voyage he had sailed by dwarfed men wearing clothes made from palms. Whenever the voyagers put the ship to land, the dwarfed men fled from the towns and made for the mountains, although the voyagers did them no harm as they went into the towns, taking only cattle away . . ." The reason that Sataspes did not voyage right around was, he said, "that the ship was not able to go on farther, but stopped." Xerxes did not believe his story. Moreover, the early and unexpected return of Sataspes had roused the king's anger, and he had him executed.

It is a strange story, and Herodotus obtained his information at secondhand while he was on the island of Samos. He heard it from one of Sataspes' eunuchs who had run away with most of his master's wealth, and was robbed in turn by a Samian. Herodotus refused to reveal the name of his informant: "I know it, but forgot on purpose."

Was the voyage just a whim of the foolish Xerxes, or was it a real attempt to explore the coast of Africa? The Persians in the time of Darius (the father of Xerxes) certainly seem to have entertained the idea of sailing around Africa. They had very likely heard of the Phoenician circumnavigation, and of the Carthaginian Hanno's voyage down the west coast of Africa (between 500 and 480 B.C.). The Persians had shown great interest in the activities of Carthage.

Necho's ships manned by Phoenicians had sailed around Africa from east to west, so why—the Persians might have thought—could the circumnavigation not be made in the opposite direction? The Carthaginians were known to have established colonies on the west coast of Africa, which assuredly meant riches were to be found there.

Herodotus's account would therefore seem worthy of belief; and the voyage may well be the first recorded attempt to sail around Africa from west to east. Sataspes, according to Herodotus,

Xerxes I

Darius punishing a rebel

190

Relief from Persepolis, showing Ahura-mazda

would have sailed along the coasts of Morocco, Senegal, and Guinea. He had clearly gone southward far enough to meet with Negro tribes beyond the Sahara, though it is unlikely that they lived in "towns." Either Herodotus or his informant had exaggerated, to make the account more absorbing. And if Sataspes reached the Gulf of Guinea, where strong northerly currents and southeasterly winds prevail, he could have said with truth that his ship would not go on. The conditions in that area often produce a flat calm. The Portuguese explorers of the fifteenth century reported that they were caught in the doldrums south of Cape Verde, and told how they just could not go farther than Cape Bojador.

Two thousand years passed before the mission given to Sataspes was successfully carried out, when the Portuguese rounded the Cape and opened the route from the Atlantic to India.

The Persian decline set in after the defeat at Salamis, and although the Persians were for a time arbiters of Greek affairs in Asia Minor, they never again attempted to invade the European mainland. The later Persian kings were weak and cruel, wielding absolute power. As the Phoenicians became aware of increasing oppression, so their doubts of the usefulness of the Persian alliance grew stronger. The first breach was when Tyre and a few other Phoenician cities secretly supported a Cypriot revolt. The governor of the island, a Greek named Evagoras, successfully defied the Persians for ten years—a sure sign of their military weakness. From time to time some Persian province

191

attempted to break away from the central authority, but despite these internal upheavals the king managed to hold his realm together by repressive measures.

A time came when the Phoenician cities—Sidon in particular —judged the moment ripe for open revolt against Persian domination, and persuaded the Egyptians to support them. This was during the reign of Artaxerxes III (359–338 B.C.). He was a younger son of Artaxerxes II, and had succeeded to the throne by inciting his father to have his three older brothers murdered. He proved to be a weak and most cruel king, thinking only of sensual pleasures, and obviously believing that the end always justified the means. Yet it must be admitted that he was fully aware of his duties as monarch. He could be energetic enough when necessary and, unlike his father, make rapid decisions and ensure that they were carried out. Sidon had not chosen a propitious time to revolt. The reigning monarch severely punished all those who tried to limit his power.

At first, however, Sidon met with success; supported by their allies, the Sidonian forces inflicted a defeat upon troops sent against them from the provinces of Syria and Cilicia. This caused Artaxerxes to fume. He raised an army of 340,000 horse and foot soldiers, and marched on Sidon. The King of Sidon, Tanes, having waited in vain for the promised help from Egypt, then saw to the fortifications of his city and mobilized its fleet of a hundred ships. The Persians had a naval force of three hundred warships and five hundred transports. Moreover, Tanes was not a particularly brave king. He began to lose heart as the vast army of the enemy drew near, and tried to save himself by acts of treachery. He caused a hundred hostages from among the notables of the city to be delivered up to the enemy. Artaxerxes at once had them killed by giving them as targets in a javelin-throwing contest. Then some five hundred inhabitants of Sidon were sent to the Persian king to implore his mercy, but they too were massacred. Tanes, in desperation, decided to buy his way into the good graces of the Persians by indicating the weak points in the city's fortifications. However, the Sidonians had stouter hearts than their king. Realizing that their only choice was between death or slavery, they made an awful decision— they first burned all the ships to prevent their falling into the hands of the enemy, then each man shut himself in his house with his family and set fire to it. Forty thousand people were said to have perished in the flames—the most spectacular collective suicide known to history. The prosperous city of Sidon was completely destroyed, and Artaxerxes sold the charred ruins

192

**Subject peoples bringing gifts
to the King of Persia**

to speculators who were hoping to discover hidden treasures among the debris.

The treachery of Tanes did not save him or his family from being put to death, though Artaxerxes did give permission for him to be buried in the tomb which he had built for himself before the revolt.

The fate of Sidon influenced the attitude of the other Phoenician cities, which by common consent put aside their plans to throw off the Persian yoke. Sidon began to rise again from the ashes; another fleet was gradually built, and the city started to recover its trade. The Persians allowed the survivor of an ancient Sidonian family to be made king. But Sidon never regained her former importance as a maritime city of commerce.

193

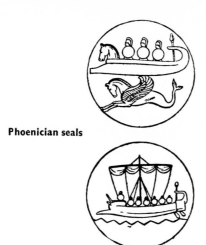

Phoenician seals

Chapter 23

THE FALL OF TYRE

King Artaxerxes III and his family were assassinated by one of their slaves. The next king, Darius III, was a weak and timid person, lacking in character. And it was he who had to face the dashing leader of an invading Greek army—a young leader, handsome as the gods, highly intelligent and of great energy, who believed he was destined to carry out the great task of creating a world empire and hellenizing it. His name was, of course, Alexander of Macedonia.

Inheriting his father Philip's power, he had as his first object the dethroning of Darius. With an army of Greeks of Macedon and of other states, he crossed the Hellespont early in 334 B.C., subdued all Asia Minor in a lightning campaign, and marched on Syria. Darius was waiting for him near the town of Issus, just south of Cilicia, with an army which has been variously evaluated by historians as between 300,000 and 600,000 horse and foot. Alexander had but 30,000. Yet he won a brilliant victory at Issus, and instead of pursuing Darius across the Euphrates he continued south into Phoenicia.

The maritime cities were taken completely by surprise; they had not expected Alexander to turn in their direction. But the strategy of the young general was quite logical. By cutting the Persians off from the Mediterranean ports he secured his rear and at the same time he ensured his sea communications with Greece. Arvad submitted at once, sending Alexander a golden crown and inviting him to enter the city. Gebal and then Sidon followed this example, and denounced their alliance with the Persians. This was no concerted move on the part of the Phoenician cities; each acted according to its own interests, naturally. Sidon sent a delegation to Alexander when he was

195

still camped some distance away. The Sidonians had not forgotten the burning of their city, and felt a deep hatred for the Persians.

Mosaic from Pompeii, showing a battle between Alexander and Darius

There remained Tyre, the most important of the Phoenician ports and the richest city of them all. The submission of Tyre would mean that the whole of Phoenicia was in the hands of Alexander, who was in fact expecting that city to surrender without a fight. Indeed, there seemed little else it could do, and a delegation led by the King of Tyre's son, Azimilk, arrived in the Greek camp. The king himself was away at sea, in command of the Perso-Phoenician navy. The delegation brought Alexander a golden crown in token of the city's submission, as well as many gifts for him and food for his troops. Alexander received the delegation in a friendly manner and assured it that no harm would be done to Tyre or the inhabitants. He added that he intended to visit the city and to make a sacrifice in the temple of the god Melkart (whom the Greeks identified with their Heracles). Alexander pointed out that he was descended from Heracles, and so it was a duty for him to a make sacrifice to the god. The fact that the temple in the island city was the

196

oldest and most renowned of the temples of Melkart gave an additional reason for a great ceremony to be held in it.

The delegation returned to Tyre and gave Alexander's message to the council of elders, who deliberated at length. Prudent and suspicious by nature, they asked themselves why Alexander should wish to sacrifice in the temple on the island, when the one on the mainland was in fact much older and more revered. Then they remembered what had happened at Ephesus, earlier in Alexander's campaign.... The Macedonian had made a similar request, except that the temple at Ephesus was dedicated to Artemis. The city had agreed, and Alexander's legions had entered with him. The elders of Tyre thought they understood Alexander's talk of a great ceremony—he meant that his soldiers would be occupying the island city!

No foreign troops had ever entered its walls, except as prisoners. The Egyptians had never succeeded in taking it, the Assyrians had besieged it for five years, and the Babylonians for thirteen, and the city had not fallen. Tyre had submitted to the Persians, but had kept its autonomy, and none of their troops had been sent to the city. If Alexander's request were agreed to, the Persians might regard it as a hostile action on the part of Tyre—the Tyrians probably doubted whether the war would end in Alexander's favor. They were aware of the immense resources of the Persian empire, whereas Alexander's comparatively small army was a long way from its base and had no fleet worthy of the name to keep it supplied. Luck had been with Alexander so far—he had gone from victory to victory—but the luck might change. The Tyrian leaders also took into account that their King Azemilcos was serving with the Persians, who might put him to death or, at best, hold him as a hostage if Tyre appeared to have gone over to the Greeks. Moreover, once Alexander was in control of the city, he might dethrone the king and replace him with someone of his own choosing.

The council's debate was long and difficult. Whatever the decision taken, Tyre would be in grave danger. There happened to be a delegation from Carthage in the city at this time; one went every year, to make sacrifice in the founder city on behalf of all Carthaginians to the gods of their ancestors. Carthage was at the height of its power and splendor, possessing a large fleet and many colonies. The Greeks were disputing the trade supremacy of the Carthaginians in the western Mediterranean, as they were that of the Tyrians in the eastern half, and Alexander was regarded first and foremost as a Greek. The Carthage delegation voted to reject his demands, and in the event of hostilities promised that Carthage would send ships and supplies to the help of Tyre. And so the council decided to oppose Alexander's entering the city.

The decision had not been taken lightly, and, contrary to the opinions of contemporary Greek historians, it was not without logic. Alexander had few ships at his command, and even if he seized those of Arvad and Gebal the Tyrian fleet would still have superiority at sea. With Carthage coming to the aid of the threatened city, its sea communications were assured. The Tyrians could evacuate the mainland population and shut themselves up in the island city, where they had already proved capable of holding out indefinitely. There was, however, one flaw to this reasoning—the Tyrians had underestimated, or not taken into account, the military qualities of this enemy and the genius of the young commander in chief. It was a mistake which was to cost them everything.

Another delegation was sent to inform Alexander that the city was prepared to submit and to accept all his terms except that of allowing him to make a sacrifice in the island temple.

Cavalry trooper in Alexander's army

Neither Greeks nor Persians would be admitted to the island city of Tyre. It was hoped that, couched in these terms, the Tyrian reply would not seem so blunt. The delegation pointed out, carefully choosing its words, that the temple of Melkart on the mainland was much older than the one on the island, and so more worthy of Alexander's ceremony.

The Tyrians sent word at the same time to King Azemilcos, informing him of the grave situation and asking him to return with as many triremes as possible, for the defense of his city. Help was probably expected from the Persians, too, as it was difficult to conceive that Darius would remain inactive when he heard the most prized jewel of his empire was in serious danger.

The attitude of the Tyrians came as a great shock to Alexander. He really believed in his divine mission, and so refused to tolerate any resistance or opposition to his plans. In his moments of anger he was capable of acts of great cruelty. He threatened the delegation in brutal terms, saying in effect that if the gates of the city were not opened to him, then he would take it by storm and destroy it utterly. But the Tyrians remained firm in their decision, and preparations were hurriedly begun to withstand a siege.

Alexander made a reconnaissance of the island, and when he saw the inhabitants on the mainland being evacuated to the island city, and realized how strongly fortified it was—in addition to the walls there were three lines of warships defending it—he knew he had a very difficult task in front of him. How were his troops to attack this island fortress when he had no ships available?

However, the Macedonian had a will of iron, and could communicate his ardor and enthusiasm to his soldiers. Only once in the course of his great military exploits were his men to refuse to advance any farther, and that was when they were already beyond the Indus and tired of battles and forced marches.

Now he assembled his officers and told them of his plan to build a causeway out to the island city. If Tyre could not be attacked by sea, then it would be attacked over firm ground! Such an audacious decision was typical of the Macedonian general, always sure of himself, never resigned to the impossible.

He would humble this proud city which had dared defy him. Besides, had he not dreamed that Heracles had opened the gates of Tyre and told him to seize the city? His astrologer had interpreted the dream—in order to capture Tyre he must first perform some Herculean task (such as building a causeway from the shore to the island city). Before putting into effect a decision which might frighten his soldiers, Alexander usually had a favorable dream or heard the oracle supporting his project. This reached the ears of his men, and was probably the most effective means of influencing them, and of convincing them that hard tasks were not imposed upon them by his will alone, but were the wishes of the gods.

In the opinion of some historians, Alexander owed his successes not so much to his strategical sense as to the bold execution of his plans and the fine example he gave to his troops. He owed it to his good luck as well, which stayed with him to the end and was greater than that of any other military commander since. All this is certainly borne out by the Greek historian Arrian, who described Alexander's campaigns in great detail.

Alexander called together his commanders and old companions-in-arms and made the following speech to them: "Friends and allies, I've learned that it would be dangerous to march on Egypt while the Persians still have command of the seas, and especially in view of the present situation in Greece. If we pursue Darius, leaving the city of Tyre unconquered, as well as Cyprus and Egypt, and if we advanced as far as Babylon, the Persians might well double back, occupy the coastal areas and throw their whole weight against Greece. Remember that the Lacedemonians have declared war on us, and although the Athenians have stayed neutral it's because they fear us, not because they like us. On the other hand, if we first capture Tyre, the whole of Phoenicia will come under our control, and the Phoenician fleet too, which is larger and better than the Persians'. It is unlikely that the Phoenician troops and seamen would then take service with our enemies, knowing that their homeland is in our hands. As for Cyprus, either it will surrender to us or we shall use our fleet to subdue it. With our own Macedonian ships and the Phoenician fleet, and very likely with ships from Cyprus too, we shall then have command of the sea, and so the conquest of Egypt will present no difficulty."

This speech shows that Alexander had indeed a wide and keen sense of strategy. The key to success was sea power in the Mediterranean—a key which would enable him to open the doors to Egypt and to the whole of the Persian empire. If Alexander had realized this when preparing his invasion of Asia, he would undoubtedly have built a fleet to support the advance of his army. But it was only when confronted with the island city of Tyre that he clearly understood the importance of a powerful navy.

The capture of Tyre had become a matter of prestige as well

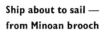

Ship about to sail —
from Minoan brooch

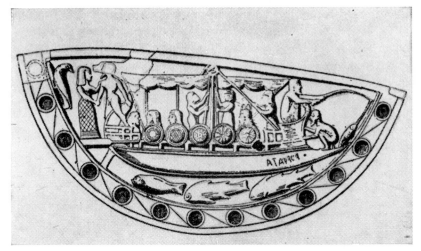

as a strategical necessity. The island city was widely believed to be impregnable. If Alexander succeeded in taking it the news would spread like wildfire all over the Near and the Middle East, and would serve as an impressive lesson to all peoples in his path. Alexander was aware of the psychological factor in warfare.

He gave orders for work to begin at once on a causeway, which would have to be about a hundred yards long to reach the nearest walls of the island city. Then Alexander would be able to send forward his powerful siege engines, the catapults and iron battering rams, to make a breach for his troops to storm. A huge quantity of rubbish and stones was cast into the channel. Alexander had the buildings and houses of the evacuated town on the mainland demolished, and their debris went to fill in the channel, but this was far from being enough. Soldiers and laborers were sent into the forests to cut down trees, which were dragged to the shore and added to the mounting debris. Other gangs were sent to quarries in the hills, to bring back stone and rubble. The local tribes frequently attacked these working parties and inflicted casualties, but Alexander organized punitive expeditions which put a stop to these attacks.

The causeway gradually increased in length, helped by the fact that the stone and rubble and tree trunks were still going into shallow waters. Alexander was said to have given a hand himself, carrying baskets of rubble on his back like any of his soldiers. At the end of a day's hard work he often distributed presents to those who had shown the greatest zeal.

However, setbacks sometimes occurred. The currents sweeping

201

through the channel carried away much of the material, and one day a storm practically destroyed all the work accomplished. But Alexander was not dismayed. He set his troops to begin again, mountains of rubble were dropped in the channel, and the deeper waters were reached.

The ship of Odysseus

The Tyrians, meanwhile, had not been inactive. The walls of the city were made higher and stronger. New engines of war were built and placed in the towers along the ramparts. Quantities of heavy stones were dumped handy as ammunition for the catapults, and every man fit for battle was issued new weapons. Tyre, in short, was ready for the fight.

Its ships made a sudden foray when the causeway had reached deeper waters. The Greek soldiers working on its construction came under a shower of arrows and stones from Tyrian archers and slingers standing in the bows of their ships. At the same time they and the crews shouted scornful remarks: "Call yourselves soldiers? Why, you're just slaves and beasts of burden!"

Such remarks were not pleasant hearing for Alexander. To protect his soldiers working on the causeway against further attack, he ordered sails and skins to be slung in front of them, to give them some shelter from missiles, and he had two wooden towers built on the causeway, and had catapults mounted in them, ready to shoot at Tyrian ships trying to draw near.

But the Tyrians had thought up a secret weapon. They loaded a ship with dry wood and other inflammable material, and hung pots of sulphur and pitch from the yardarms of two tall masts fitted in the bows. Boulders and heavy stones were placed in the stern, so that the bows would be lifted high out of the water. When a strong westerly wind started to blow, the Tyrians shook out the sails and sent this fireship heading toward the wooden towers on the causeway, having set light to torches and made sure the flames were spreading.

Her bows riding high, the blazing ship was blown against the towers, setting fire not only to them but also to tree trunks and branches embedded in the causeway. Many of the soldiers in the towers and those working at the end of the causeway were badly burnt. Others who jumped into the water were killed by arrows or captured by the Tyrians. To make matters worse for the Greeks, the wind strengthened to gale force, aiding the flames, while the raging waters tore at the gap made in the causeway and broke up much of its length.

The months of hard work by thousands of men had to be started all over again—such were Alexander's orders. Profiting from experience, he ordered trees complete with their branches and leaves to be dragged into the channel, then stones, rubble and earth heaped on top of them, and more complete trees spread over the whole. Defense towers were built as the causeway progressed—faster now. Alexander worked with his men, encouraging them all through the winter. By the beginning of spring the causeway had almost reached the island.

Alexander began to assemble his siege engines along the shore, and the Tyrians realized that urgent measures were needed. Being ingenious people, they again hit on a successful method. Their best swimmers went and secretly examined the causeway, and discovered that iron stakes had been driven through it and into the sea bed. They returned to fetch ropes, which they fastened to the stakes, then pulled. They succeeded in bringing away part of the construction. Other bits followed, and soon a length of the causeway collapsed sideways and broke up.

This fresh setback convinced Alexander that he would get nowhere without the support of a fleet. While the Tyrians held command of the sea they could always parry his efforts; and he could not starve them out, being unable to hinder the Carthaginian ships that brought them supplies.

His excellent intelligence services gave him the information that a number of ships which had deserted the Persian fleet had just sailed into Sidon. Alexander went there, his luck still held. The combined fleet of Arvad and Gebal had succeeded in slipping away from the Persians. He at once opened talks with the two commanders and convinced them of the desirability of joining him. With the Sidon ships, he thus had a fleet of eighty under his control. This was hardly enough, but soon ships rallied to him from other parts. Rhodes, which had turned against the Persians, sent him a dozen triremes. They were followed by thirteen ships from Lydia and Cilicia. Alexander's homeland, Macedonia, responded to his appeals by sending him a ship, one solitary ship.

While Alexander had been without ships, the small maritime powers had hesitated to join him. When they knew he had gathered a fleet together, however, they were quick to rally to his support and get into his good graces. Cyprus in particular, seeing which way the wind was blowing, abandoned the Persian cause, and its whole fleet of one hundred and twenty ships appeared off Sidon, at the disposal of Alexander.

He then had a total naval strength of two hundred and twenty-four ships. Moreover, he received reinforcements of about four thousand soldiers just then, recruited in Greece by his agents. For the most part they were well-trained mercenaries, attracted by the prospect of loot from the rich cities of the East.

Alexander now had the means of completing the causeway under the protection of ships. But first he embarked some of his troops, to train them for a sea fight. The Tyrians must have been greatly surprised, and dismayed, when the enemy fleet appeared off the island. Alexander had obviously found fresh allies, and the fate of Tyre was in the balance. Before the blockade of the island city became effective, some of the women and children were evacuated to Carthage. Not for a moment did the Tyrians think of capitulating. They avoided a full-scale naval battle, however, and endeavored by various stratagems to gain time, hoping that the Persians would come to their aid. But Darius had no interest in the fate of Tyre; he had given up all idea of reconquering the Mediterranean seaboard. The Tyrians made a boom of boats and ships at the entrance to each of their two harbors, to deny the enemy access, and prepared to fight to the death.

Alexander was therefore obliged to continue work on the

204

Coin of Darius III

causeway. Progress was slow. The summer heat reduced the men's capacity for work, and the besieged kept inventing new means of hindering the work and inflicting casualties. In addition to shooting arrows and hurling stones, they began sending across "bombs" made of sand and burning tar, using catapults erected on the city ramparts. These forerunners of modern incendiaries caused almost equally painful wounds. The Tyrians also choked and blinded the workers with thick smoke, and bombarded the wooden towers on the causeway with lumps of red-hot iron. Nevertheless, the causeway increased in length. Alexander was as determined as the Tyrians were obstinate.

He then used his ships to try to batter at the walls of the island fortress, by placing siege engines on the decks and ordering the crews to anchor alongside the ramparts. But the defenders lowered great stone blocks to the foot of the walls, preventing the enemy ships from drawing too near.

Alexander had learned some tricks from the Tyrians. He sent divers down to attach ropes to the stone blocks, so that ships could haul them away. But then Tyrian divers cut the ropes, and the anchors of the enemy ships too, causing them to be driven against the walls by the wind and current. Alexander made another attempt, using iron chains. Thus one measure met with countermeasure, and hatred engendered hatred.

The causeway was again almost completed, and the Tyrians prepared for the worst. They made their ramparts even higher, and built a second, inner wall where the defenses were weak. When the causeway was only a few feet from the wall, they began to lower long hooks and kept trying to wrench away bits of the material, and to cast nets in the hope of hauling up a few of the enemy working to finish the causeway. Several were in fact trapped in these nets and pulled up to the top of the ramparts, where they were most cruelly killed in sight of their comrades.

Alexander was preparing a combined attack by sea and across the causeway. But first he tried to provoke the Tyrians to a naval battle by dividing his fleet into two squadrons, sending the Cypriot ships to cruise off the northern harbor of the island and himself leading the remainder to anchor outside the southern harbor. The Tyrians, however, dared not take the risk of a pitched battle. Their situation was becoming desperate. Ships from Carthage were no longer able to get through with supplies, and food was running short in the besieged city.

There seemed no prospect of any Persian intervention. The only hope was to force the blockade. The Tyrians decided to mount a sudden attack on the Cypriot fleet moored outside the

205

northern harbor. They hid their preparations by stretching sails across the harbor entrance, then filled thirteen ships with their best fighting men. In the middle of the day, when the enemy was either eating or dozing, the Tyrians dashed out of the

Ancient Roman lamp, with picture of Alexandria harbor

harbor, rowing furiously, and were in among the Cypriot ships before their crews realized what was happening. Many ships were sunk, others went aground on sandbanks. All was going well for the Tyrians, until Alexander sent off some ships which were anchored near the shore; while they went to the help of their comrades, he brought the rest of his fleet around from south of the island. The Tyrians in the thirteen ships were too hotly engaged to notice the approach of Alexander's squadron. Nor did they at once grasp the significance of the signals made by the Tyrians watching the whole scene from the ramparts. The Tyrian ships became hopelessly outnumbered, their retreat was cut, and all thirteen were either sunk or captured. However, many of the fighters succeeded in swimming to the island.

The gallant attempt had not met with the success hoped for, but the besieged still did not think of surrendering. Alexander's ships sailed around the island, continually bombarding the walls with missiles from their catapults and trying to approach near enough to anchor and batter away with their iron rams. The defenders lowered skins stuffed with seaweed to reduce the effect of the blows, and poured burning sand on attackers who came within reach. But eventually a small breach was made in the southern wall, and Alexander prepared to carry out a general assault on the island city. He divided his fleet into four groups. Two were to attack the harbors while a third continued circling and bombarding the walls. The fourth, consisting of only two ships commanded by Alexander in person, would then attempt to storm the breach. He embarked the best of his veterans, the tried and proven warriors who had set off with him from Macedonia to carve out an empire. The seaborne attack was to be supported by a land assault over the causeway built at the cost of many lives and long effort.

It was mid-July when this combined attack was delivered. The small force with Alexander succeeded in getting a gangway across to the breach and fighting a way into the city. Admetos, the captain of one of the ships, was killed, but Alexander pressed on, using his sword to great effect and inspiring his men. He seemed to bear a charmed life, to have some divine protection, and his courage and daring undoubtedly contributed greatly to the success of the attack. The defenders began to give ground, for the enemy ships had penetrated into both harbors and put a number of troops ashore. The Tyrians defended their city street by street, house by house. It was a merciless, bloody battle. The Greeks had not forgotten the hideous deaths of their captured comrades, and were able at last to avenge them.

207

Many of the Tyrians made a last stand in the temple of Astarte, in the main square of the city. Alexander directed the attacks on it, and when the building was forced all the defenders were put to the sword. Other Greek soldiers were massacring the inhabitants street by street. Eight thousand Tyrians met their death in this way, and another two thousand captured sword in hand were hanged by order of Alexander. He spared only the lives of those who had taken refuge in the temple of Melkart; this was Alexander's tribute to the god.

Thirty thousand Tyrians, men, women and children, were sold into slavery. Alexander was immensely proud at having captured, in less than a year, the city which had defied the Assyrians for five years and the Babylonians for thirteen. He celebrated his victory with a military parade outside the temple of Melkart, and made sacrifice to the god as he had decided at the very beginning. And in gratitude to Heracles, from whom he claimed descent, Alexander presented the god with the great iron battering ram which had made the first, all-important breach in the walls of Tyre.

Alexander began his march on Egypt with every feeling of satisfaction. Not a single living inhabitant was left in the ruins of Tyre, and the news of its fall was spreading far and wide. Tyre, the pearl of the Levant, had possessed the finest fleet and had boasted of the greatest tradition of independence in the ancient world—but Alexander had crushed all that, had stamped out its brilliant splendor and wiped its beauty from the face of the earth. Who would now be foolish enough to resist him?

An idea of Alexander's vanity can be gained from the following account by the historian Arrian:

"Soon after the fall of Tyre, Darius sent envoys to Alexander, offering him an enormous sum of money to make peace; Darius also offered to give his own daughter in marriage to Alexander, with a dowry of all Persian territory south of the Euphrates. These attractive proposals were considered by Alexander's council, and one member declared that if he were Alexander he would accept the Persian king's offer. 'If I were Parmenio [one of Alexander's generals],' replied Alexander, 'I should accept too!'"

This reply, like the refusal he gave to the Persian envoys, was evidence of his clear thinking and youthful assurance. If he needed money, any amount was his for the taking, and similarly with women—if he wanted Darius's daughter, he had no need of the King's permission. As for the territories south of the

208

Euphrates, the whole of the Persian kingdom was now at his mercy.

Alexander's attitude was soon supported by facts. The only city to oppose him on his march south was Gaza, which fell after a siege. The entry into Egypt followed. He founded the city of Alexandria, which became a great international port, a center of learning and the chief market for all the people of the East. For the proud city of Tyre was no more; its ships were no longer met with at sea, nor its caravans on land.

Alexander the Great

Chapter 24

LAMENT, YE SHIPS OF TARSHISH!

The few Tyrians who had survived the massacre returned to their ruined city and began the task of rebuilding. Even the sea, usually so bent on destruction, gave what help it could. The waves added sand and shingle to Alexander's causeway, which became quite a wide roadway linking the island to the mainland. But the proud spirit of the city was forever crushed. Tyre, queen of the seas, had vanished and would not return; her scepter and her creation, the fleet, had been destroyed and her trade ruined. However, Tyre did make an effort to regain her former importance after Alexander's death, but was always under the domination of one power or another.

A dynamic energy had created and sustained the ancient city during a thousand years of glory and prosperity. She had been "the crowning city, whose merchants are princes," and was

211

indeed "perfect in beauty." Her people had been the elite among the Phoenicians. But Isaiah's doleful prophecies had come true... "Lament, ye ships of Tarshish. For it is laid waste, so that there is no house, no entering in .... Howl, ye inhabitants of the isle ... the Lord hath given a commandment against the merchant city, to destroy the strongholds thereof."

After the wailings came silence, a deep silence which lasted for generations. The Tyrian harp, which according to Isaiah had made such sweet melody, lay at the bottom of the sea, silent forever. Phoenician ships continued to ply between many lands, but they were no longer the wondrous vessels of Tyre and Sidon, but those of the daughter city Carthage, the rich and powerful colony that flourished in the West.

Tyre, Sidon, Gebal, and Arvad had played their part. Now their bold ventures, their shipbuilding yards and their amazing expeditions were nothing but memories. The whole of the ancient world had benefited from the initiative and energy of the Phoenicians in general and the Tyrians in particular. They produced no great scholars or artists, but were above all enterprising men of business, capable of great heroism when their liberty and independence were threatened. The sea was their domain, and their outstanding merit was their practical ability. They made great advances in shipbuilding, and were fine seamen. Only the Greeks were ever better, and that was after many centuries of endeavor. For a long time the Greeks merely followed in the wake of the Phoenicians.

The Phoenicians were fine traders and craftsmen. After their decline it was long before any people attained their standards in copperwork, weaving and the dyeing of cloth. By their trading enterprises the peoples of the East and the West were brought into contact; they were the links by which others attained a higher standard of living. They were greatly imbued with the spirit of adventure, and were lured on by the mysterious unknown. It was instinct just as much as the hope of material gain which made them undertake long sea voyages. Their ships sailed all over the Mediterranean, and were the first to venture into the Atlantic. They explored the Indian Ocean and the coasts of Africa. They penetrated the northern mists to reach the shores of England and Ireland. The Phoenicians thus showed that man is able to overcome great obstacles, to conquer vast expanses and confront the wild elements. Although they were realists and practical men, the Phoenician epic is filled with poetry, with the heroic songs of men daring the wild waters of the unknown. A great period in maritime history ended with the fall of Tyre.

212

ALASTIOS, D. *Cyprus in History.* London, 1955

APOLLODORUS. Loeb Classical Library, 1946

ARISTOTLE. *Politics*

ARRIAN. *Anabasis.* Tr. J. Chinnock, N.Y., 1942

AVIENUS. *Ora Maritima.* Ed. by A. Schulten, Barcelona, 1922

AYOOB, J. C. *Were the Phoenicians the First to Discover America?*
The Compiler Aliquippa., 1950

BAIKIE, J. *The Sea Kings of Crete.* London, 1910
The Amarna Age. N.Y., 1926

BARR, S. *The Will of Zeus.* Philadelphia, 1961

BAUMANN, H. *The World of the Pharaohs.* N.Y., 1960

BEATTY, CH. *De Lesseps of Suez.* N.Y., 1957

BEAZLEY, C. R. *The Dawn of Modern Geography.* 3 vols. Ed. by
Peter Smith, N.Y., 1949

BENNETT, H. TH. *The Pylos Tables.* Princeton, 1955

BENWELL, G. *and* WAUGH, A. *Sea Enchantress.* London, 1961

BOLAND, C. H. *They All Discovered America.* N.Y., 1961

BREA, L. B. *Sicily Before the Greeks.* London, 1958

BREASTED, J. H. *Ancient Records of Egypt.* Chicago, 1906
*The Development of Religion and Thought in
Ancient Egypt.* N.Y., 1912
The Dawn of Conscience. N.Y., 1936
History of Egypt. N.Y., 1950

BROWN, R. *The Story of Africa and its Explorers.* 4 vols. N.Y., 1911

BUDGE, E. A. W. *The Rise and Progress of Assyriology.* London,
1925

BUNBURY, E. H. *A History of Ancient Geography.* London, 1879

BURGH, W. G. DE. *The Legacy of the Ancient World.* London, 1947

BURN, A. R. *Minoans, Philistines and Greeks.* London, 1932

BURTON, H. E. *The Discovery of the Ancient World.* Cambridge,
Mass., 1932

213

CABAL, J. *Piracy and Pirates. London,* 1957

CARPENTER, R. *The Greeks in Spain.* Brynmawr, 1925

CARY, M. *and* WARMINGTON, E. H. *The Ancient Explorers.* London, 1929

CASSON, L. *The Ancient Mariners.* N.Y., 1959

CATON-THOMPSON, G. *The Zimbabwe Culture.* Oxford, 1931

CHAPIN, H. *and* SMITH, F. G. W. *The Ocean River.* N.Y., 1953

CHATTERTON, E. K. *Battles by Sea.* N.Y., 1925

CHILDE, V. G. *The Dawn of European Civilization.* N.Y., 1927
    New Light on the Most Ancient East. N.Y., 1957
    What Happened in History. London, 1960

CHILDERS, E. B. *The Road to Suez.* N.Y., 1961

COTTRELL, L. *The Lost Pharaohs.* N.Y., 1951
   Life under the Pharaohs. N.Y., 1955
   The Mountains of Pharaoh. N.Y., 1956
   The Bull of Minos. London, 1957
   The Anvil of Civilization. London, 1958
   Wonders of Antiquity. London, 1959

DAVIDSON, B. *The Lost Cities of Africa.* Boston, 1959

DOBLHOFER, E. *Voices in Stone: the Decipherment of Ancient Scripts.* London, 1961

DOUGLAS, J. S. *The Story of the Oceans.* N.Y., 1952

DUNBABIN, T. J. *The Western Greeks.* Oxford, 1948

DURANT, W. *The Story of Civilization: our Oriental Heritage.* N.Y., 1935
   Life in Greece. N.Y., 1939

EDGERTON, W. F. *Ancient Egyptian Ships and Shipping.* Chicago, 1933

EDWARDS, J. E. S. *The Pyramids of Egypt.* London, 1955

ERMAN, A. *A Handbook of Egyptian Religion.* London, 1907
   The Literature of the Ancient Egyptians. London, 1950

EVANS, A. *The Palace of Minos in Knossos.* 4 vols. London, 1921-1936

FORDE, C. D. *Ancient Mariners.* London, 1927

FORSDYKE, E. J. *Minoan Art.* British Academy, 1929.

FRANKFORD, H. *Birth of Civilization in the Near East.* N.Y., 1956

FREEMAN, E. A. *History of Sicily from the Earliest Times.* Oxford, 1894

FREEMAN, O. W. *Geography of the Pacific.* London, 1951

FREUCHEN, P. *Book of the Seven Seas.* N.Y., 1957

GLOVER, T. R. *Herodotus.* Berkeley, 1924
   The Ancient World. London, 1957

GLUECK, N. *Rivers in the Desert.* N.Y., 1959

GRAVES, R. *The Greek Myths.* Vol. 2, London, 1955

GROSECLOSE, E. *Money and Man.* N.Y., 1961

HALL, E. H. *The Decorative Art of Crete in the Bronze Age.* Philadelphia, 1907

HALL, H. R. *Aegean Archeology.* London, 1915
        The Ancient History of the Near East. London, 1927

HAMMOND, N. G. L. *A History of Greece.* Oxford, 1959

HARDEN, D. *The Phoenicians.* London, 1962

HAYNES, E. B. *Glass through the Ages.* London, 1959

HERODOTUS. *The Persian Wars.* Tr. Rawlinson, N.Y., 1942

HERRMANN, P. *Conquest by Man.* N.Y., 1954

HURST, E. H. *The Nile.* London, 1957

HYDE, W. W. *Ancient Greek Mariners.* N.Y., 1947

KAY, F. G. *The Atlantic Ocean.* London, 1954

KERENYI, C. *The Gods of the Greeks.* London, 1951

LANDSTRON, B. *The Ship.* London, 1961

LEIP, H. *The Gulf Stream Story.* London, 1957

LISSNER, I. *The Living Past.* N.Y., 1957

LONGGOOD, W. F. *Suez Story.* N.Y., 1957

LUDWIG, E. *The Nile: the Life Story of a River.* N.Y., 1937

MCCRINDLE, J. W. *The Commerce and Navigation of the Erythrean Sea.* Calcutta, 1879

MARTIN, A. *Tartessos.* Seville, 1940

MASON, G. *Columbus came Late.* N.Y., 1931

MASPERO, G. *The Dawn of the Nations.* London, 1903
        The Struggle of the Nations. London, 1910

MEIGS, J. F. *The Story of the Seaman.* 2 vols., Philadelphia, 1924

MELA, POMPONIUS. *De Choragraphia*

NILSSON, M. P. *The Minoan-Mycenean Religion.* Lund, 1927

NILSSON, M. P. *and* OLMSTEAD, A. T. *History of Palestine and Syria to the Macedonian Conquest.* N.Y., 1931

OLMSTEAD, A. T. *A History of the Persian Empire.* Chicago, 1948

ORMEROD, H. A. *Piracy in the Ancient World: an Essay in Mediterranean History.* London, 1924

OUTHWAITE, L. *The Atlantic: a History of an Ocean.* N.Y., 1957

PALMER, L. R. *Myceneans and Minoans.* N.Y., 1962

PAUSANIAS. *Description of Greece.* Tr. J. G. Frazer, London, 1898

PAVER, B. G. *Zimbabwe Cavalcade.* London, 1957

PAYNE, R. *The Canal Builders.* N.Y., 1959

PENDLEBURY, J. D. S. *The Archaeology of Crete.* London, 1936

PLINY, THE ELDER. *Historia Naturalis.* Loeb Classical Library

PETRIE, W. M. FLINDERS. *Tel-Amarna.* London, 1894
        History of Egypt. London, 1914-1924

PRITCHARD, J. B. *Ancient Near-Eastern Texts.* Princeton, 1950

RANDALL-MACIVER, D. *Medieval Rhodesia*. London, 1906
                     Greek Cities in Italy and Cicily. Oxford, 1931
RAWLINSON, H. *The Phoenicians*. London, 1889
RAWLINSON, H. G. *Intercourse between India and the Western World from the Earliest Times to the Fall of Rome*. Cambridge, 1926
ROSE, J. H. *The Mediterranean in the Ancient World*. Cambridge, 1933
ROSTOVTZEFF, M. *History of the Ancient World*. Oxford, 1930
SAVAGE, G. *Pottery through the Ages*. London, 1959
SELINCOURT, A. DE. *The World of Herodotus*. Boston, 1962
SHEPARD, A. M. *Sea Power in Ancient History*. Boston, 1924
SMITH, G. *The Cassiterides*. London, 1863
STRABO. *Geographia*. Loeb Classical Library
SYKES, P. *A History of Exploration*. London, 1949
TARN, W. W. *Alexander the Great*. Cambridge, 1951
THOMSON, J. O. *History of Ancient Geography*. Cambridge, 1948
THUCYDIDES. Loeb Classical Library
TORR, O. *Ancient Ships*. Cambridge, 1894
TOUSSAINT, A. *Histoire de l'Ocean Indien*. Paris, 1961
TOZER, H. F. *History of Ancient Geography*. Cambridge, 1935
VAUGHAN, A. C. *The House of the Double Axe*. N.Y., 1959
VILLIERS, A. *Monsoon Seas: the Story of the Indian Ocean*. N.Y.-Toronto, 1952
WACE, A. J. B. *Mycenae: an Archeological History and Guide*. Princeton, 1949
WARMINGTON, B. M. *Carthage*. London, 1960
WARMINGTON, E. H. *Greek Geography*. London, 1934
WEBSTER, T. B. L. *From Mycenae to Homer*. London, 1960
WOOLLEY, L. *Ur of the Chaldees*. London, 1929
                Digging up the Past. London, 1940
XENOPHON. *Anabasis*. Tr. Dakyns, N.Y., 1942
           Hellencia. Tr. Dakyns, N.Y., 1942